BETWEEN
TWO LOVES

BETWEEN TWO LOVES

DEVOTIONS
FOR WOMEN
WHOSE HUSBANDS
DON'T SHARE
THEIR FAITH

NANCY KENNEDY

GRAND RAPIDS, MICHIGAN 49530 USA

We want to hear from you. Please send your comments about this book to us in care of zreview@zondervan.com. Thank you.

ZONDERVAN™

Between Two Loves
Copyright © 2003 by Nancy Kennedy

Requests for information should be addressed to:
Zondervan, *Grand Rapids, Michigan 49530*

Library of Congress Cataloging-in-Publication Data
Kennedy, Nancy, 1954–
    Between two loves : devotions for women whose husbands don't share their faith / Nancy Kennedy.
        p. cm.
        ISBN 0-310-24848-5
    1. Wives—Religious life. 2. Marriage—Religious aspects—Christianity.
3. Husbands—Religious life. I. Title.
BV4528.15.K455 2003
242'.6435—dc21   2002154349
                                                CIP

This edition printed on acid-free paper.

All Scripture quotations, unless otherwise indicated, are taken from the *Holy Bible: New International Version®*, NIV®. Copyright © 1973, 1978, 1984 by International Bible Society. Used by permission of Zondervan. All rights reserved.

Published in association with the literary agency of Ann Spangler & Associates, 1420 Pontiac Road SE, Grand Rapids, MI 49506.

Interior design by Todd Sprague

Printed in the United States of America

03 04 05 06 07 08 09 /❖ DC/ 10 9 8 7 6 5 4 3 2 1

Contents

INTRODUCTION

If I were God, I would do things differently. I would make brussels sprouts sinfully fattening and glazed donuts mandatory for optimum health. Take two in the morning with hot tea.

If I were God, I would not allow chin whiskers on women . . . and whenever a person came to faith in Christ, his or her spouse would too—preferably at the same time. Two for the price of one. After all, the two are one flesh.

If I were God, there would be no such thing as an unequally yoked marriage. No going to church alone, no arguments over teaching the kids to pray.

No spiritual chasms.

No feelings of despair.

No pining for what could be or thoughts of "How long, Lord, before you answer my prayer?"

The problem is, I'm not God. That means it's the glazed donuts, not the sprouts, that are sinfully fattening, and middle-aged women do grow unsightly facial hair.

That means too that some marriages remain spiritually unequal—some for months, some for years, some for decades, some for life.

A pastor friend of mine often reminds me that his grandmother prayed for his grandfather for forty years before he became a Christian. He tells me that so I might be encouraged to not give up praying for and loving my own husband, who is not yet a believer.

Some days it's easy. We're laughing and horsing around on the living room floor. We're sharing a bowl of popcorn or strolling around Home Depot looking for lawn sprinklers. We're sitting on the back porch talking about the future.

But other days it's not so easy. Jesus gets in the way. I ask one too many times, "Will you come to church with me?" Or I turn a simple discussion into a one-sided sermonette, which turns into an argument.

The very thing I want to do—share my faith with the one I love most on earth—is the very thing that seems to drive us farther apart.

I feel guilty and frustrated.

I feel lonely and misunderstood.

Angry and rejected, confused and discouraged.

Not always . . . but often enough to wonder if I'll ever reach a point where my faith is strong enough and my hope sure enough to keep me from this emotional roller coaster.

Have I described your life? If so, be encouraged: You're not alone. The churches are filled with women just like you and me who engage in a constant tug-of-war between two loves: God and husband.

It doesn't seem right that there has to be a choice. It's hard to get up each Sunday morning and be pulled in two opposite directions. *Do I stay home or go to church yet one more time alone?* You want to please your husband—you want to enjoy him and be his wife and friend. You also want to please God. You want your husband to join you . . . but he doesn't see the need. Or he's hostile to the whole idea of faith.

Dear friend, God knows your struggle. He sees. He hears your cries and your sighs. He holds your prayers close to his heart, saving them for his glorious answer . . . someday.

Meanwhile, God is doing something in your life that's beyond what you can dream. Something amazingly good! After all, he promised:

- that if he began a good work in you, he will complete it (Philippians 1:6).
- that his plans for you are to (spiritually) prosper you and not harm you, to give you a hope and a future (Jeremiah 29:11).
- that he will never leave you or forsake you (Hebrews 13:5).
- that he will give you strength to do all things (Philippians 4:13) and sufficient grace for every weakness (2 Corinthians 12:9).
- that he is able to do immeasurably more than all we ask or imagine, according to his power that is at work within us (Ephesians 3:20).

Funny thing about God, though. He promises to do all these amazingly good things in your life, so you naturally assume his plans include answering your prayers for your husband's salvation. After all, if you were God, that would make the most sense. The *best* thing, or so you think, would be the two of you loving Christ together, serving God together, raising your children in the Lord. *Together.*

But God's ways and plans aren't the same as yours and mine. His are so much grander in scope and impact. His are complete. Ultimate. Total.

And always, always, always good.

I don't know why God allows some marriages to be spiritually unequal. Some are a result of a rebellious choice to marry an unbeliever. Yet for those who do so, there is always forgiveness. A Christian marrying an unbeliever is always mistaken, but the marriage that results is not a mistake as far as God is concerned. Even then, God is still in charge.

But what about the rest? What about the marriages between two unbelievers that the Lord invades, calling one spouse into a relationship and leaving the other one as he is? Even then, God is in charge.

As I said, I don't know why God does what he does. I only know he has a reason for everything and asks us to trust that he knows what's best: for us, for our children, for our husbands, for our marriages, for our present, and for our future.

> Even when things are hard . . .
> Even when things look dark . . .
> Even when it feels as if the gates of hell have opened up
> and dumped on your house . . .

Even then, God is still in charge. His plans are still good. He still knows what he's doing and he will do what's best for you and me in order to make us fit for his kingdom.

He's active and alive. He's at work—don't you ever forget it. And he's more than able to take care of you.

He also wants you to know that he's given you and me everything we need to prosper in this life through his Word and through the privilege and power of prayer.

Through his Word God reminds us of his deeds and shows us a portrait of his Father-heart. We're strengthened and encouraged. Our minds are renewed.

Through prayer we share our hearts with him. We curl up on his lap and pour out our hurts to the only One who can turn them into joy.

The fervent prayers of God's children are powerful and effective, writes the New Testament writer James (James 5:16, my paraphrase). Some translations use the words "avails much." They benefit greatly. If nothing else, our prayers draw us close to our God, and we gain spiritual empowerment. We rise from our knees a little (or a lot!) more confident—not in ourselves, but in the One who holds the universe securely in his grip.

Plus, in God's great plan, he may even use our prayers to accomplish his will. So, he invites—he compels—us to pray, and he tells us that Jesus himself is praying for us as well (John 17:9).

I wrote this book as one wife of a not-yet-believing husband to another. I know what you're facing. I know your struggles and loneliness. I know your excitement over the tiniest glimmer of spiritual progress and the disappointment at ground seemingly lost.

I know how desperately you need hope and encouragement, because I need it too.

That's the purpose of this book. Each short entry gives a verse of Scripture, an application, and a prayer—bite-sized for those times when you need encouragement *fast*. Please note too that many of the names used in the devotions have been changed for obvious reasons.

As you read, keep in mind that I'm praying for you. I'm praying with you. Remember, we're in this together: you, me, and the Lord who called us into this honored position as Christ's missionaries within our own marriages.

It's an awesome calling. But then, he's an awesome God . . . an awesome God who is able to keep you from falling and to present you before his glorious presence without fault and with great joy (Jude 24).

To him be honor and glory! Amen.

THE GEOMETRY
OF FAITH

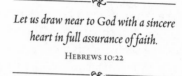

*Let us draw near to God with a sincere
heart in full assurance of faith.*

HEBREWS 10:22

I had been a Christian for a few years when I joined a prayer group with three other young moms my age—and a brash nineteen-year-old named Kenny. Reluctant to study the Bible and put what little I did study into practice, Kenny constantly chided me for holding back in my faith. At the time, I was concerned that my relationship with the Lord was driving my husband and me apart, and I was afraid if I drew any closer to God, it would cause an even bigger rift. To me, it made more sense to wait until Barry joined me in the faith, and then we could draw closer to the Lord together.

Kenny disagreed.

To prove his point, he drew an equilateral triangle on a piece of paper and labeled the top point GOD and the base points HUSBAND and WIFE.

"The closer you move toward God, the closer you'll be to your husband," he said.

I thanked him for his insight, but I didn't believe him. What did some nineteen-year-old kid know about marriage? When I got home, I took out my ruler so I could prove him wrong.

But the kid was right.

Geometrically speaking, a husband and wife are never farther apart than when they're both at the base. And even if only one person moves toward God, the distance between the two spouses decreases.

When a believer is married to an unbeliever, there's always the temptation to hold back, to wait for the other one to come along. But the truth is, unless you move forward, you actually move farther away.

"Draw near to God and he will draw near to you" (James 4:8 RSV). Draw near to God, and trust that you'll be drawn closer to your husband as well.

Loving Father,
It wasn't always like this—
This distance between my husband and me.
I miss him. I long to be close to him again,
Yet I long to be close to you as well.
Once again, I'm feeling torn. And afraid.
You're bidding me to draw near to you
And promising that if I do, you'll draw near to me too.
Although I long to have my husband join me so we can draw
*   near together,*
Ultimately, we each stand before you on our own.
When I hold back from you, I miss out on so much that you have
*   for me—*
Love and patience, peace and joy, wisdom and strength—
All the gifts that enable me to draw near to the one I love.
Thank you, Lord. I see much more clearly now.
Draw me nearer, my precious Lord.
Amen.

Is My Marriage a Mistake?

ᕲᕲ

Yet who knows whether you
have come to the kingdom for
such a time as this?

ESTHER 4:14 (NKJV)

ᕲᕲ

Nobody gets married with the desire to live *unhappily* ever after. We stand next to our beloved and promise to love each other:

> *For better* ("We'll have such fun!")
> *For worse* ("How bad can it get? Our love will see us
>   through")
> *For richer* ("A four-bedroom house will be perfect")
> *For poorer* ("We'll survive on macaroni and cheese")

You know the rest.

But we probably never planned on one day having our lives radically changed by faith in Christ—and we never, ever imagined the resulting spiritual chasm.

Then one day we find ourselves wondering if our marriage was a mistake. We ask, "Are my kids being harmed because their dad makes fun of my faith? Wouldn't it be better to get out now and find a Christian to marry?"

However, the question isn't, "Do *I* think my marriage is a mistake?" but "Does *God* think it's a mistake?"

In their book *What If I Married the Wrong Person?* Dr. Richard Matteson and Janis Long Harris point out that dwelling on

15

whether or not you married the right person ignores God's stake in the choice you already made.

No matter whom we chose to marry, it didn't take God by surprise. Not only that, *even if we did make a mistake,* God is more than able to take it and use it as part of his higher plans for us, our husbands, our children, their children, and so on.

God knows what he is doing. He never says "Oops." So, next time you start thinking that your marriage is a mistake, consider this: It just might be that God has placed you with *this* man at *this* time for his kingdom purpose.

From eternity's perspective, it's not a mistake. It's a call to service.

Lord,
When I look at my life—at my marriage—
Sometimes it's hard to remember that none of this
Took you by surprise.
It's easy to forget that everything
Is from your all-wise and loving hand.
You who keep the stars in place knew what you were doing
When you placed me with this man.
He's the husband you have given me.
Even if we married because of a sinful choice
Being married isn't sinful.
It's not a mistake either, because you don't make mistakes.
Thank you, Lord, for in that I can rest.
Rest . . . and be confident that all things,
Even my most foolish choices,
You will work together for good.
You've promised it.
Please keep reminding me, Lord.
It's so easy to forget.
Amen.

My Husband's Bible

You are a letter from Christ ...
written not with ink but with the
Spirit of the living God, not on tablets
of stone but on tablets of human hearts.

2 CORINTHIANS 3:3

M y friend Jerry calls it "Annie's flying Bible." Now that he's
a Christian, he laughs about it, but ten years ago he says
it wasn't at all amusing to find his wife's Bible "mysteriously"
appear everywhere he went throughout the house—open and
with key verses highlighted for his benefit. He couldn't even go to
the bathroom without finding her Bible on the back of the toilet!

He says he felt hounded, and that made him more determined to avoid reading it.

Rick, another now-Christian husband, says he also resented
his wife's attempts at "pushing" the Bible on him. It made him
feel like a "bad" boy and as if she was his angry mother scold-
ing him.

"Every other sentence out of her mouth began, 'The Bible
says.' I eventually tuned her out," he admits. "When she started
preaching, I went out to my workshop to get away from her."

Keeth, on the other hand, says he read his wife's Bible faith-
fully—he read her life.

Now a Presbyterian pastor, Keeth was an atheist when his
wife gave her life to Jesus. Since he was so vocal about his dis-
dain for Christianity, Lori never said a word to her husband.

However, he read the changes in her life.

He admits he would go on anti-God tirades. Then whenever Lori would go out, he would take her Bible down from the bookshelf and read it until she came home. Keeth says reading Lori's life first made him want to read more from the book that was responsible for the changes he saw in his wife.

Dear Father,
It's your Word that brings faith.
"Faith comes by hearing . . . the Word of God."
But getting my husband to read it—
Well, it's easier to pull a mule that's stuck in the mud.
I worry, Father, that he will never hear the Word!
That he will never come to faith.
You tell me to be quiet,
To live the Word, not preach it.
Not push it.
That whatever I do, whether I'm silent or pushy and obnoxious,
Either way, I'm preaching with my life.
If the adage is true—
That I may be the only Bible my husband will ever read—
Then I want my life to reflect your wonderful words of grace.
May your Word dwell in me richly!
Amen.

HE IS MIGHTY
TO SAVE

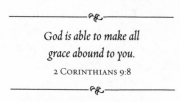

*God is able to make all
grace abound to you.*

2 CORINTHIANS 9:8

A s a religion reporter for my local newspaper, I've written hundreds of Christian testimonies. Each one a living illustration of the grace, sovereignty, and creativity of our God. "He is mighty to save," the prophet Zephaniah wrote. How true!

Each interview leaves me in awe of how God works in the lives of those on whom he sets his love. I'm struck by how no two testimonies are alike, and how God is not limited to saving people through a church service, a sermon tape, a seminar, or the Four Spiritual Laws.

He doesn't even need *me*.

There was a time I thought he did need me to get my husband's attention. After all, who knows him better than I do? Who else knows what pushes his buttons? Who better to explain the gospel in a way he'll comprehend? But all my best efforts seemed to fail. My words fell on deaf ears. My "subtle hints" were ignored.

I worried because he didn't have any Christians in his world. I tried to figure out ways to get him into church. I left gospel tracts on the seat of his truck. I felt personally responsible for his spiritual condition.

Then, one day, I thought about my own conversion. No one (other than God) had pursued me. No one had evangelized me. As far as I know, no one even prayed for me. No one invited me to church. I didn't hear a sermon tape, watch Christian TV, listen to Christian radio, or read a Christian book.

Yet God saved me, using two words painted on the side of a blue van to capture my attention: "Jesus Saves." Eventually, those words became my prayer: "Jesus, save me!"

The more I'm reminded of my own testimony, the more I'm reassured that God is mighty to save even my husband—without my help. He may choose to use me, but he may not. Either way, he is more than able to make all grace abound. To you, to me, to the ones we love.

Gracious Lord,
Truly your ways are higher than mine.
Your knowledge of my husband is far greater,
Your plans so much more perfect.
Once again
I come to you confessing my doubts,
Admitting that I think I know best—
Even though my best efforts to bring about my husband's
    salvation
Only get in the way of what you want to do.
I limit you.
I've put you in a box,
Thinking that you can only work this way.
But you tell me simply
To be still and know that you are God—and I am not.
May my thought for today be this:
You are able and you are good.
Blessed be your name.
Amen.

THE GOSPEL
AND THE WWE

---

*My prayer is not that you take them
out of the world but that you protect
them from the evil one.*

JOHN 17:15

I t's a Monday night. Your husband grabs a beer and a bag of chips and plops down on the couch to watch wrestling. He's pumped—he loves this stuff.

Meanwhile, you grab a diet soda and your Bible and close yourself off in the kitchen or bedroom. You think you're being obedient to God by keeping yourself from "secular" influences and setting a Christian example to your husband. However, in your zeal to be in the world but not of it, you end up alienating your husband. Whether you intend to or not, you convey the message: "Christians think they're too good."

So what do you do? You don't like wrestling (or sitcom reruns or vulgar talk shows), and you want to honor the Lord. But you don't want to isolate yourself and appear "too good" to associate with your husband. You feel conflicted. You want to do the right thing—if only you knew what that was!

May I suggest something? First, strike the word "secular" out of your vocabulary. As a child of God, anything you do in service to him in accordance with his Word is sacred. Sitting with your husband as he watches wrestling is sacred. You're doing what Jesus would do. You're entering into the world of one who needs Christ's love.

That doesn't mean you do anything that violates God's Word. The Lord doesn't expect you to go to an X-rated movie or to a drug party. You don't even have to become a wrestling fan, just a fan of your husband.

So next time, instead of hiding in another part of the house with your Bible, take a magazine or crossword puzzle into the living room and sit next to the one God gave you to love. And don't worry about being influenced by evil. Jesus already prayed for you—and he continues to pray.

And the Father always answers his prayers.

Father,
You know my heart,
That I long to fill my mind with "psalms, hymns and spiritual
*   songs"*
And keep myself undefiled.
But you've called me to be in my husband's world.
It's hard, Lord!
Especially when his world is so different from mine.
I don't like feeling separate—
And I know he views my wanting to be spiritual
As condemnation of him.
Forgive me, Father,
For in many ways he's right.
I have looked down on him.
Replace my self-righteous heart with a God-righteous one,
A heart like Jesus,
Who ate and drank with "sinners," and did so out of love.
Oh, may I love like that!
Amen.

THINK ON
THESE THINGS

---

*Your attitude should be the same
as that of Jesus Christ.*

PHILIPPIANS 2:5

You're ticked. While your husband's at work, you've spent the entire day reviewing every one of his faults, real and imagined, particularly dwelling on every slight, every slur, every snide remark he's ever uttered against you and your faith. He thinks the Bible is full of myths and the church full of hypocrites.

By the time he comes home you've built your case against him and conclude he's the lowest form of pond slime on earth. As he grabs the mail and asks, "What's for dinner?" you shoot him an icy stare, storm off in a huff, or tell him exactly what kind of jerk you think he is.

At best, he's left confused, wondering what he did wrong. At worst, it leads to a fight—all because you let your thought life rule your attitude, which ruled your actions. As the proverb goes, "For as he thinks in his heart, so is he" (Proverbs 23:7 NKJV).

It's a common temptation for women in spiritually unequal marriages to dwell on what they consider to be their husbands' spiritual shortcomings. When that happens, it leads to every kind of evil.

The good news: With every temptation, God provides a way of escape to keep us from sinning. In this case, it's taking every thought captive. Next time you start dwelling on thoughts that tear at your husband's character, give them instead to Jesus. Say, "Lord, while it's true that my husband (makes fun of my faith, etc.), thinking about it will only lead me to act unloving and disrespectful toward him. So I give this thought to you."

But don't stop there. Next, choose something you admire about your husband and think on it. Not only will this please the Lord, but your husband will notice as well.

Gracious Lord,
It's true—my thoughts toward my husband
Color my attitude and my actions toward him.
If I think, "He's a jerk,"
If I think, "He's unfair,"
If I think, "He's nothing but an ungodly heathen,"
And dwell on what I don't like,
Then I become the jerk; I become the ungodly one.
Forgive me, Lord!
I give you all my wayward thoughts—
All my anxious ones too.
Help me to replace each one with whatever is true and noble,
*   right and pure.*
Whatever is lovely, admirable, excellent, or praiseworthy,
Whatever is good in my husband,
Help me to think on these things.
For your glory.
Amen.

GUARD YOUR HEART

Above all else, guard your heart,
for it is the wellspring of life.

PROVERBS 4:23

When it comes to male-female relationships, is there anything less discerning than a lonely heart? You know how it goes: He's someone in your Sunday school class, a Christian coworker, someone you met on-line.

You strike up a conversation and think, *At last—here's someone I can talk to about my faith!* To you, he's a heaven-sent answer to your spiritual loneliness. He genuinely cares about you and your walk with God. He asks about your husband, offers to give you a man's perspective, tells you he's praying for you.

Everything between you is above board. *He's just a brother in Christ,* you think. What could be more innocent? What could possibly be wrong?

Guard your heart!

It's a fine line between innocent fellowship and emotional adultery. All it takes is revealing one secret, sharing one private detail, receiving one sympathetic response. Your lonely heart—the wellspring of your life—begins to be stirred. You give more, receive more. You make him your confidant. He understands. He knows your God!

But what began in innocence crosses that fine line. Even if no physical contact between the two of you takes place, you've given your heart to another man. At best, it merely eats you up inside. At worst, your husband senses someone has come between you—and he's hurt . . . and angry.

So, guard your heart:

- Acknowledge your vulnerability. Be aware of potential danger.
- Never make a man other than your pastor or a counselor a confidant. Even then, be on guard.
- In mixed fellowship gatherings, stay in a group. Avoid one-on-one discipleship with a man.
- Cultivate your friendship with your husband. Find common ground between the two of you.
- Go to God *first*. He alone can meet your heart's deepest needs. He alone satisfies.
- Pray that God will keep you from evil.

Father,
You know me so well!
You made me a woman, with a need for emotional connection
    with a man.
You made me with this longing
To share myself—to share my spiritual self.
Oh, Lord! How easily I fall into the trap
Of sharing myself with the wrong person.
Even when it seems right; even when it seems innocent.
But you know me all too well.
Help me, Lord, to guard my heart.
Give me discernment . . . and wisdom.
Open my eyes to the emotional danger around me,
That I may be spared the pain of falling.
Help me instead to find ways to connect with my husband
And find my ultimate satisfaction in you.
For your glory I pray.
Amen.

TIME WILL TELL

❦

But when the time had fully come,
God sent his Son.

GALATIANS 4:4

❦

Now he's a pastor, but ten or so years ago Ed Jones was just a regular guy who attended his kids' ball games, partied on the weekends, and loved his wife.

For all of their married life, his wife took their kids to church without Ed. Christianity was OK for her, but he didn't want any part of it. He didn't challenge her; he just didn't think he needed saving.

This went on for more than twenty years. Ed knew Mina was praying for him, but even that didn't affect him.

Then one night he woke up crying. He kept saying, "Thank you, Lord," and "Praise you, Jesus." He said at that moment he knew he had given his heart to Christ, and he's never been the same since.

He told me this to make a point. As a pastor, he sees women fretting and worrying and nagging their husbands over their lack of a faith commitment. As a husband on the "being prayed for" end of things, he's experienced a wife's desire to have her husband a part of God's kingdom.

Although he credits his wife's faithfulness and diligence in praying for him, he says it wasn't until *God's time* that he was able to respond to the Spirit's tug on his heart.

"That should give a woman comfort," he says.

Jesus told his disciples, "No one can come to me unless the Father has enabled him" (John 6:65). Similarly, the apostle Paul wrote, "It does not, therefore, depend on man's desire or effort, but on God's mercy" (Romans 9:16). Unless the Spirit is at work, unless it's God's time, no amount of words, prayers, pleading, or tears can bring a man to faith.

"So you just relax," Jones says. "Be faithful—and love that husband of yours. God's not done yet. It's all in his time. You just wait and see."

Lord,
Thank you for the comfort of your Word
Reminding me that you make everything beautiful in your time.
Thank you that one day to you
Is like a thousand years—and a thousand years like just
    one day.
You choose the appointed time
For everything.
You're never early; you're never late.
How wonderful to know that I can rest in that!
Father, I believe you have a plan
And in your perfect timing it will come to pass.
Meanwhile, help me to stay faithful
In prayer and in my actions
As I love my husband and wait for you.
Amen.

BLESSED ARE
THE FLEXIBLE

---

*It is for freedom that Christ
has set us free.*

GALATIANS 5:1

When we lived in California, my husband did some restoration work on an old house in San Francisco, about a hundred miles north of where we lived. Nearly every weekend he would go up there early on a Saturday or Sunday morning, usually by himself.

One weekend, however, he decided it would be fun if I and our two daughters went with him as a family outing. But because he had to work on Saturday, Sunday was the only day we could go.

It happened to be Easter Sunday.

My heart sank. Family outings were scarce, but going meant missing church—on Easter Sunday at that. (Of course, I would have preferred if we all went to church together, but that wasn't an option.) It was either stay home and go to church while Barry went to San Francisco alone, or miss church and go with my husband.

You better believe I prayed about that one! And then I made my choice: Family outing.

As it turned out, it was probably one of the best times we ever had as a family. Not only that, we listened to a tape of praise music on the way up and talked about Jesus. On the way home we went out for Mexican food and said grace together at the table.

It was a day blessed by God. He had known my heart and how I longed to experience worship on that holy day—and he arranged for it to take place, albeit in a most nontraditional way.

My pastor at the time used to say, "Blessed are the flexible, for they shall not be broken." We are free in Christ, not bound by rigid rules. The commandment is to love God and keep his day holy, and while we shouldn't make a habit of skipping church, there is flexibility in Christ. It's called grace.

"Commit your way to the LORD; trust in him and he will do this: He will make your righteousness shine like the dawn" (Psalm 37:5–6), wrote the psalmist. Who knows? He may even give you an Easter worth remembering.

Father,
You have set me free in Christ
To love and serve you,
Even—especially—within my unequally yoked marriage.
I can trust that you will guide me
And help me to make the right choices.
You know my heart.
You see my dilemmas.
You will come to my rescue and my defense
And bless me beyond my expectations.
Even if I make a wrong choice, your grace covers me.
Your grace, abundant and amazing, sets me free.
Thank you for granting me freedom.
In Jesus' name.
Amen.

LOVE FOR
THE LEAST

If anyone says, "I love God,"
yet hates [her husband, she] is a liar.

1 JOHN 4:20

I have a friend who hates her husband—at least she did. Even after she became a Christian a few years ago, she still felt only contempt for him. Her only happy moments were when he was out of town.

At the same time, she was excited about her new faith, and she loved loving God. Then she heard her pastor say, "You only love God as much as you love the person you love the least."

She said when she heard that, her face got hot and she felt sick to her stomach. She knew exactly whom she loved the least, and it pained her to think that that was the measurement for her love for God.

After some thinking and much praying, she decided she needed to do something. It wasn't easy, but after months of not having any physical contact with her husband, she offered him a hug. She said he stiffened at first, not sure what was going on, but then he relaxed and returned an awkward hug of his own.

"But that's not the most amazing part," she said. "After I hugged him, I told him I loved him—and I meant it!"

I rejoiced with her. This is big stuff.

Even under the best circumstances, love isn't easy. However, when natural affection dies and faith drives an even deeper wedge between a couple, sometimes love seems nearly impossible. But as my friend has discovered, a woman who thinks she can love God and continue to hate her husband is fooling herself.

Fortunately for us, God knows something about loving the unlovable. And because he loves us first, we can draw from that love and share it with others. Even those we love the least.

Father,
Somewhere on the way to happily ever after
Some of us got lost.
We lost love. We lost hope.
Not only that, we discovered it's easier to hate or feel nothing.
It's easier to stay this way than to risk changing.
Besides, once love is lost . . .
Well, the word "impossible" comes to mind.
However, you say no one can love you
While at the same time hate a brother (or a husband!).
That's a grievous thought.
But even then, you've made a provision
To supply love where there is none.
Thank you for your love, Lord!
For it is great indeed.
Amen.

Rx FOR
DISAPPOINTMENT

---

*No good thing does he withhold from
those whose walk is blameless.*

PSALM 84:11

Everything falls into place. You've prayed like crazy and now it's time to pop the question: "Honey, would you like to go with me to the (sweetheart dinner/marriage seminar/church picnic/Bible study/Easter service)?"

He says yes! (Or at least "maybe.") As the day approaches, he still hasn't backed out—neither has the baby-sitter, and everyone has stayed healthy. You're so excited you can barely contain it. You've waited months, maybe years, for your husband to show an interest in spiritual things.

Then at the last minute something goes wrong. The car breaks down, a storm hits, your husband changes his mind. The specifics don't matter; you're not going and you're disappointed beyond description. And you're angry. You had your hopes up, and now they've been dashed. You feel as if a cruel joke's been played on you.

What do you do? How do you deal with your disappointment without sinning—without taking it out on your husband?

I've found the perfect answer: Psalm 84:11, which says, "No good thing does he withhold from those whose walk is blameless."

33

As I see it, because God does not withhold any good thing from those whose walk is blameless—from those who are blameless in Christ—then quite possibly the thing I wanted was not a good thing for me, at least not at that time. If it had been a good thing, then God would not have withheld it. Since he knows best, I can trust every outcome to his sovereignty. Thank you, Lord!

It's the best and quickest way I know not only to ease disappointment, but also to change it into thanksgiving.

> *All-knowing Father,*
> *You are too wise and too kind*
> *To be arbitrary in your dealings with me.*
> *That's why I know—I'm confident—that this thing I wanted*
>   *so badly*
> *Was not a good thing for me.*
> *You know my disappointment, and I know your love for me.*
> *Thank you, Lord!*
> *Even though I don't understand, I don't have to.*
> *I only have to trust that you know best.*
> *So, I give you this disappointment and exchange it for*
>   *thanksgiving.*
> *Thank you, Father, for your loving care for me.*
> *Amen.*

THE SANTA CLAUS
WAR

--------- ❧ ---------

Love is patient, love is kind ...
it is not rude, it is not self-seeking.

1 CORINTHIANS 13:4–5

--------- ❧ ---------

One of the worst faith-related fights my husband and I ever had was over Santa Claus. At the time, I was an obnoxious, zealous new believer getting ready for Christmas. Our daughter, Alison, was only two at the time, and I was eager to teach her about the birth of Baby Jesus. My husband was equally eager to teach her about Santa Claus.

In my zeal to keep my house free from all "secular" influences, I adamantly opposed anything Santa-related. Any mention of his name and I would immediately go to work "deprogramming" my daughter.

To my husband's credit, he suggested we allow Santa *and* Jesus in our holiday celebrations, but I wouldn't even consider it. *No child of mine is going to be forced into pagan practices.*

It created a stand-off and a terribly uncomfortable Christmas season as we lobbed angry bombs at each other. Thankfully, a wise older woman at church took me aside and gently told me I was at fault in the Santa Claus War. She told me I needed to choose my battles with loving discernment, and Santa Claus wasn't worth the destruction of my family.

Instead, she suggested a compromise that wouldn't compromise biblical standards: Treat Santa the same as Mickey

Mouse and Big Bird—fun, but make-believe. Besides, St. Nicholas was an historical figure who worshiped Jesus, she pointed out.

After I apologized to my husband for my pig-headedness, we called a truce and ended the war. He was right; we could have Santa *and* Jesus after all.

Lord,
You know how I desire to do what's right.
To teach my children your ways and to keep them from worldly
    influences.
But too often my desires get clouded by emotion.
I shoot my mouth off before I take the time to think things
    through,
Or to seek your wisdom.
You know how much I don't want to compromise my faith,
But these aren't just my children; they're my husband's
    children too.
Thank you, Lord, that you already know that,
and you know just what I should do
In every situation.
Even when it comes to dealing with Santa Claus.
Help me, Lord, I pray.
In Jesus' name.
Amen.

SUNDAY'S COMIN'

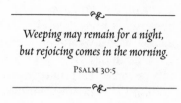

Weeping may remain for a night,
but rejoicing comes in the morning.

PSALM 30:5

I remember lifting my head off my pillow and laying it back down with a thud. Months before, my beloved husband of twenty-five years had plunged into a dark depression, turning from his usual even, good-natured self into a sullen and angry stranger. The night before, he had talked about leaving, and when I woke up, he was gone. I didn't know when or even if he would be back. Married for more than half my life, I faced an unknown future alone. It was Saturday, and I was in a Saturday kind of mood.

In the gospel records, the Saturday before that first resurrection morning, the disciples, too, were in despair. Jesus had died the day before, and they were grief-stricken and despondent. Their hope had died along with the One they had thought would change the world. Everything looked bleak. Dark. Dead.

Have you ever felt that way too? You don't see any spiritual progress in your husband, or maybe even in yourself. Your marriage seems to be disintegrating before your eyes. Your faith is cold.

God is silent.

All you can do is cry; you can't even pray.

On Saturday, you don't see any signs of salvation, and the devil seems to dance.

37

For a moment, for a Saturday, I had lost hope. The only thing that got me through that day was a message I had heard on the radio years before. I don't remember the preacher's name, but I still remember his words: "When all hope is gone, when everything looks black, when Jesus is in the grave—get ready, because Sunday's comin'." Only he said it like this: "Sundaaaaaaaaaaaaay's ah-cominnnnnnnnnn!"

On Sunday, the dead rise to resurrected life. Hope is reborn and restored. Sorrow turns to unspeakable joy. That's Sunday. And for God's people, Sunday always comes.

For me, Sunday came slowly. My husband returned, but he didn't come out of his depression until several months later. It was Saturday for a long time, but I held on for Sunday.

If it's Saturday for you, I'm sorry. But remember, for God's people, Sunday always comes. How do I know? Because in a garden somewhere in Jerusalem there's an empty tomb where a body lay dead one Saturday. Then Sunday came.

So, if you're down, if hope is dead, if it's Saturday for you, remember: Sunday's comin'. And Sunday will come again.

Almighty God,
On that Saturday morning, when everything looked beyond hope,
When Jesus was dead, and the disciples grieved . . .
You knew.
You knew that Sunday was coming, that Christ would arise,
And lives would be changed.
Ever since that day, you've been changing lives, changing
marriages—
Changing entire families.
And even though I'm feeling low, I trust that you are changing mine.
Because Sunday's comin'!
It may feel like Saturday right now, but hallelujah, Sunday's
a-comin'.
Amen!

WHEN THE DEVIL WALKS IN THE DOOR

---❧---

*For our struggle is not against flesh
and blood, but against the rulers,
against the authorities, against the
powers of this dark world and
against the spiritual forces of evil
in the heavenly realms.*

EPHESIANS 6:12

---❧---

E verything's fine. You're enjoying your day, looking forward
to your husband coming home. You've even fixed his
favorite dinner.

You're all "prayed up." Your faith is secure. Then your husband walks in . . . and it's as if the devil walked in behind him.

Maybe you start it. Before doing anything else, he grabs a
beer, and you can't help thinking how much you hate his drinking and how, if only he were a Christian, your family life would
be so much better. That's when you say something you immediately regret. ("What kind of an example are you setting for our
kids when you do that?")

Or maybe he starts it. He walks in, hears the Christian radio
station that's on in the kitchen, and says, "That's a crock. You
have to be brain dead to believe that."

You hurl an insult at him, shoot him a disgusted look, turn
a cold shoulder.

By this time, it really doesn't matter who started it; right now your home has become a war zone. Furniture isn't flying around the room, but you're sure a spiritual battle is being waged.

What do you do now?

The first thing you do, especially if you're at fault, is stop and apologize. "Honey, I'm sorry. I'm wrong—I shouldn't treat you like this."

If he starts it, resist the urge to strike back.

Next, find a quiet place (even if it's just in your thoughts) and cry out to God for help. Call on Jesus' name and trust that he will answer. Then negotiate a cease-fire if possible. Add some humor. ("Let's rewind the tape and start over.") Tell a joke; put on some music. Offer your husband a compliment—or a sandwich.

Take a deep breath; smile if you can.

Remember, your *husband* isn't the enemy, although your real enemy wants you to think he is. Don't fall for it!

Finally, turn your arsenal on your real enemy, the devil, and tell him to flee.

Father,
I shouldn't be surprised when spiritual battles occur;
They only mean that you're at work.
But often I am surprised and I feel ambushed, blind-sided.
That's because when the devil walks in, he doesn't announce
himself beforehand.
Even so, you haven't left me without a remedy.
You've said, "Resist the devil and he will flee."
You've said your Spirit in me is greater than my enemy,
And you've given me spiritual weapons with which to fight
spiritual battles—
Not against my husband, but for him.
He's not my enemy; he's my husband.
Thank you, Lord.
Amen.

A LOVE
THAT DOES

❧

Let us not love with words or tongue
but with actions and in truth.

1 JOHN 3:18

❧

Love isn't easy, not even if your husband is a committed Christian. My husband works out of town during the week, and it's easy to love him perfectly ... when he's gone. We get along great ... in my imagination. I talk to him daily and generally am on my best behavior ... over the phone.

But when he's home and our lives bump against each other, sometimes we create an uncomfortable friction. It's during these times, when the loving feelings aren't there, when misunderstandings get between us, or when the Holy Spirit is at work convicting one or both of us of sin and tempers are easily ignited, that love gets tested.

During those times when love doesn't *feel*, that's when love *does*.

Love sacrifices. It puts aside pleasure, position, power, or prestige for the benefit of another person.

Love acts. It cooks and cleans and folds laundry for its beloved (even when that's the last thing it wants to do). Love goes to softball games and bowling tournaments; it gives back rubs and pulls weeds.

Love speaks. Its words are kind and uplifting. Love never gossips, belittles, blames, or tears down.

Love respects. That doesn't mean blindly approving of another person's actions, but respecting the other person's being. Love looks for the positive and prays about the negative. Love offers hope to the hopeless.

Love holds on. It stays, even when tempted to leave. It perseveres; it endures.

Love never fails.

God of love,
In myself I don't possess an unfailing, enduring love.
I don't naturally respect; my words and actions are often unkind.
Where love should be patient, I am impatient.
Where love should not be self-seeking, I want my own way.
I am easily angered and often keep records of wrongs.
But your love, Lord, is perfect—toward me, toward my
    husband, toward our marriage.
Your love is a "doing" love,
And it's that very love that enables me to "do" love the way
    I should.
Not that I need to muster up that love (because I can't),
But to draw on your unlimited supply.
So, fill me with that love, Lord,
And point me toward my husband.
In your name.
Amen.

WIND OF
CHANGE

The wind blows wherever it pleases.
You hear its sound, but you cannot
tell where it comes from or where
it is going. So it is with everyone
born of the Spirit.

JOHN 3:8

Where I live in Florida, it's rarely windy except down by water. Several years ago we lived in a condo on a lake, where I enjoyed many breezy late afternoons and evenings.

At times, everything would be still. Then, without warning, a strong gust would whip across the water and shake the Spanish moss out of the oak trees on the bank of the lake. But then, just as quickly as it came, the wind would either shift or die down altogether.

When I was out by the lake, I loved to feel the wind on my face. It reminded me of Jesus' words to Nicodemus, "So it is with everyone born of the Spirit."

It's tempting to keep our eyes on an unbelieving husband for signs of God at work in his life. We monitor progress: *He's close. He's not close. God's drawing him. God's forgotten him.* Our moods rise and fall with the "signs" of the Holy Spirit's moving.

However, we don't know, and we can't predict, when and how God will act. It could be with a whisper of a breeze—one day your husband quietly decides to give his life to Christ. It could be with the force of a mighty hurricane—a crisis brings

43

him to his knees. In either case, it's God who directs the wind, and it's God who directs how and when a person comes to faith.

"No one can come to me unless the Father . . . draws him," Jesus told his disciples.

No one comes unless the wind blows. Just as we cannot control or predict the wind, neither can we control or predict the Spirit's moving. We just wait and pray that it blows our way.

Father,
Thank you for earthly reminders of spiritual truths.
I can't control my husband's spiritual life any more than I can
   control the wind.
But you can, and you do.
And I can pray.
I do pray—that you will send the mighty wind of your
   Holy Spirit into my husband's life.
Into my life.
Into our marriage.
Gently as a breeze, mightily as a gale,
Whatever it takes—
Blow, Lord, blow!
Amen.

SET APART
FOR BLESSING

— ❧ —

For the unbelieving husband
has been sanctified through
his [believing] wife.

1 CORINTHIANS 7:14

— ❧ —

Did you know that your unbelieving husband has a privileged position in God's eyes? The apostle Paul told the believers in Corinth not to divorce an unbelieving spouse who is willing to stay, because that spouse has been "sanctified."

That word means several things. "Sanctified," as it pertains to believers, means separation from evil things and ways. Another definition is "made holy." God is making us better every day. "Sanctified," as it pertains to unbelieving spouses and children, means "set apart." Because of the covenant relationship God makes with believers through Christ, he extends his blessing to include a "setting apart" of a believer's immediate family.

Every individual must make his or her own Christian commitment. This verse doesn't promise an instant, all-inclusive, family-pack salvation. It does, however, promise God's special attention. As the Lord blesses me, his child, the blessings spill over onto my husband.

During my pregnancy with our youngest daughter, my husband was unemployed. Some of the countless ways the Lord took care of us back then included the church stocking our kitchen with groceries several times, church members anonymously giving us large sums of money, and a few church people even hiring my husband to do odd jobs while he looked for permanent employment.

God's provision for me as his child didn't exclude my husband. In that way, my husband reaped the benefits of my relationship to Christ, and he saw first-hand the amazing grace of God to his covenant people. He has since looked back on that time and acknowledged that God, indeed, was good to us.

He continues to be, and my husband continues to see.

What a great and generous God!

Gracious God,
You never cease to amaze me!
How merciful and kind you are.
Thank you for reminding me that you haven't left my husband
out in the cold.
You have included him in your plans for my life,
Including its blessings.
May he know it, even right at this moment,
That you have set him apart.
You "set the lonely in families" (Psalm 68:6).
You redeem the ones who are lost.
Remembering that and recalling all the ways you show
your personal love
To me and my family
Bring great comfort.
Thank you, Lord.
Amen.

How To WOW
Your Husband

---

*In the same way, you wives, be
submissive to your own husbands so
that even if any of them are disobedient
to the word, they may be won without
a word by the behavior of their wives.*

1 Peter 3:1 (NASB)

I'd just given the most eloquent theological monologue known to Christendom. I had spelled out in minute detail the plan of salvation and even threw in a few Bible chapters and verses about a husband's role. When I had concluded, I looked at my husband sitting at the kitchen table and said, "Well?" (meaning: "Well, have I convinced you yet?").

He didn't say a word. Just stared into space. I could tell he had tuned me out completely. I changed the subject and asked him if he wanted a sandwich. *That* he heard.

Later, as I vented and fumed at God for my husband's lack of response to my many words, I thought I heard God say, "WOW him."

Gee, Lord. I thought that's what I was doing.

However, God meant WOW him as in, "without words." Stop talking. Zip it. Shut your mouth—and keep it shut.

I've come to the conclusion that God knows more about men than I do. He knows that unlike women, who are verbal by nature, men are not. And for whatever reason, a man is persuaded more by his wife's behavior than by anything she says.

Do you want to WOW your husband? Then do it without a word. Do it by your godly, loving behavior. If you do, he'll hear you loud and clear.

Father,
I don't understand why you tell me not to speak to my husband
     about my faith
When you know that's what I want to do most!
That's the natural thing.
Being quiet is unnatural.
For me to do so would be . . . supernatural.
But I trust you, Lord,
When you say that's how I'm to be.
I also trust that you will give me opportunities to speak,
But speak sparingly . . .
In your power and not my own . . .
And for your glory.
My prayer is that you would place a guard over my mouth
So that my actions
Will speak louder than my words ever could.
In all I do, may your glory shine, I pray.
Amen.

A CLEAR GLIMPSE
OF GOD

───────── ❧ ─────────

*In the same way, let your light
shine before men, that they may
see your good deeds and praise
your Father in heaven.*

MATTHEW 5:16

───────── ❧ ─────────

In his book *Revolution Within*, Dwight Edwards reminds Christians that we were and are called, saved, justified, and sanctified for God's glory. He adds that God makes "New Covenant promises" to every believer and places within each of us four revolutionary provisions: a new purity, a new disposition, a new identity, and a new power. Edwards also encourages believers to approach life in a radically different manner from what is "normal," thus shaking up people's perspectives on God. "The bottom line: Give others a clearer glimpse of God," he writes.

In everyday life with an unbelieving husband, what does that look like? First of all, it stems from an unwavering core conviction that God has already equipped us with whatever we need to live a God-reflected life, and that what most glorifies him is *not* teeth-clenching obedience to a set of principles but an obedience motivated by grace and gratitude. We *want* to do as we *should*. The exciting news, as Edwards points out, is that God has provided us with the "wants" for his "shoulds."

We know we shouldn't lie, we shouldn't gossip, but now we actually want not to do it. We want not to cheat on our tax forms; we want not to steal candy from the open bins at the market. We are no longer motivated by a fear of getting caught but by a genuine desire to please God. To an unbelieving world, that's not "normal." Without the Spirit's indwelling a person, he or she cannot please God and doesn't desire to do so.

Therefore, when an unbelieving husband observes his wife willingly going the extra mile, instinctively returning a kind word in response to his harsh ones, and giving of herself sacrificially and joyfully, especially when she hasn't wanted to do so in the past, he gets a clear glimpse of what God can do in a life that belongs to him.

A God who changes desires and provides a new purity and a new disposition, a new identity and new power—that's the God the world hungers for.

That's the God we want our husbands to see.

God of grace,
Deep within me
I long to bring glory to you with my life.
That is my purpose—
You created me for your glory.
First. Foremost.
In all that I do, as I do it unto you,
Your Word says all will see and give you thanks.
I pray that my life
Will be a reflection of your life within me,
That my husband will see that the Christian life
Is lived out of gratitude to a glorious God
And is not a life based on graceless, rigid rules.
In my life, Lord, be glorified.
Amen.

A Wife Deserted and
Distressed in Spirit

—❦—

The LORD will call you back
as if you were a wife deserted
and distressed in spirit.

ISAIAH 54:6

—❦—

E ven if you've done everything right, even if you've loved God with all your strength, and even if you've reflected that love to your husband, even after years of good times and laughter, your husband just might decide he doesn't want to be with you anymore.

Maybe there's someone else. Maybe he wants to pursue wild, prodigal living. Maybe he simply withdraws his affections. When he sees Christ in you, it reminds him of his own emptiness, and he can't bear it . . . so he retreats.

And you're hurt. You're confused.

You think it's all your fault.

Or, you blame God. *Marriage isn't supposed to be like this*, you think. *I want happily ever after!*

Listen to what your Father says in Isaiah 54:5–6:

"For your Maker is your husband—
    the LORD Almighty is his name—
the Holy One of Israel is your Redeemer;
    he is called the God of all the earth.

The LORD will call you back
    as if you were a wife deserted and distressed in spirit—
a wife who married young,
    only to be rejected," says your God.

This is not a guarantee that your marriage will ever be heaven on earth. We're only promised heaven in heaven. Instead, this is a glimpse into God's heart for you today, and his promise that he will be for you everything that you long for in a husband. He'll be everything you need.

He's your True Husband.

Run to him. He's waiting just for you.

Jesus,
You know how I feel, don't you?
You were deserted and distressed in spirit.
You know how it feels to be rejected.
Just as I feel right now.
I hurt, Lord!
I look at my husband and long for him to hold me,
Love me,
Want me, and cherish me.
But he doesn't.
Oh, God! (That's all I can say right now.)
Oh, God!
You who will never desert me,
I offer you my hurting heart.
Be for me what I need most:
My Lord, my King, my Husband, my Friend.
Amen.

IF ONLY . . .

---

*We take captive every thought
to make it obedient to Christ.*

2 CORINTHIANS 10:5

We all need hope. We need a goal, a vision, a dream. Each one of us desires a husband who shares our faith—and we should. That's a biblical desire. That's God's desire. He doesn't want anyone to perish but all to repent (2 Peter 3:9).

However, our God-given, God-shared desires easily become unbalanced. We think:

If only my husband was a Christian . . . he would serve me breakfast in bed and always wipe off the bathroom sink after he shaves.

If only my husband was a Christian . . . we would go to every church event; our kids would behave; he would sing me love songs.

If I start pinning my hope of fulfillment and happiness on my husband's salvation instead of on God, salvation becomes an idol in my life. I'm saying in essence, "The source of my happiness is in my husband's becoming a Christian."

Not only that, "if only" thinking colors my behavior toward my husband. Because "if only" thinking is often unrealistic, it disappoints. Others always fall short, and we react accordingly. Loudly and clearly they hear the message, "You're not good enough the way you are," even if we don't utter a single word.

The best remedy for "if only" thinking is to take each thought captive and give it to the Lord, and then to replace it with "here and now" reasons to give thanks.

In your marriage, what are you thankful for today?

> Lord,
> The truth is,
> Even though I am a Christian,
> I fall short of being the ideal wife.
> My husband probably has "if only" thoughts of his own!
> Forgive me, Lord,
> For placing expectations on my husband and our marriage
> That are not only unrealistic, but self-centered.
> How easily I forget that you—and you alone—
> Are ultimately what my heart desires most.
> If only I would remember that!
> I thank you for my husband, just as he is.
> Open my eyes to his good qualities,
> That I may change my "if only" thinking to thanksgiving.
> Thank you for my husband.
> Amen.

IN CHRIST, I AM . . .

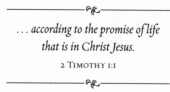

*. . . according to the promise of life
that is in Christ Jesus.*

2 TIMOTHY 1:1

How easy it is to forget who we are in Christ, especially for those in an unequally yoked marriage. Even those who have walked with the Lord for decades need daily reminders of the incredible riches of God's grace for those he calls his much-loved children.

Here's a reminder for today that in Christ, I am:

Redeemed, cherished, and deeply loved.

Therefore, as God's chosen people, holy and dearly loved. . . . (Colossians 3:12)

New.

Therefore, if anyone is in Christ, he is a new creation; the old has gone, the new has come! (2 Corinthians 5:17)

Able to do all things God requires of me.

I can do everything through him who gives me the strength. (Philippians 4:13)

Safe.

If you make the Most High your dwelling—even the LORD, who is my refuge—then no harm will befall you, no disaster will come near your tent. (Psalm 91: 9–10)

Free.

It is for freedom that Christ has set us free. (Galatians 5:1)

God's workmanship.

For we are God's workmanship, created in Christ Jesus to do good works, which God prepared in advance for us to do. (Ephesians 2:10)

Where God wants me.

And who knows but that you have come to royal position for such a time as this? (Esther 4:14)

Clothed with Christ's righteousness.

. . . not having a righteousness of my own that comes from the law, but that which is through faith in Christ—the righteousness that comes from God and is by faith. (Philippians 3:9)

Invited to approach God's throne.

Let us then approach the throne of grace with confidence, so that we may receive mercy and find grace to help us in our time of need. (Hebrews 4:16)

The bride of Christ.

"Come, I will show you the bride, the wife of the Lamb." (Revelation 21:9)

My Father,
In Christ, I am your child!
I am set apart, loved, safe.
Not because of anything I have done
But only because of what Christ has done for me.
You say in your Word
That my real life is hidden in Christ,
And in Christ, I am yours.
In Christ, I have been given all things.
How easy it is to forget.
Thank you for your faithful reminders in your Word.
I am yours.
I am yours.
In Christ, hallelujah! I am yours!
Amen.

THE POWER IN PRAYER

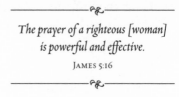

*The prayer of a righteous [woman]
is powerful and effective.*

JAMES 5:16

W hen I was a new Christian, I thought all I needed to do was deposit a certain number of prayers for my husband's salvation into a prayer bank account, and when it got to a predetermined amount, *cha-ching!* God would grant me my answer.

I remember staying awake for hours one night praying over and over, "Lord, save him. Lord, save him." When the morning came and my many prayers went unanswered, I felt discouraged. *Obviously, I haven't reached the magic number,* I thought.

In my naiveté at the time, it was the only way I knew how to pray. No one had shown me another way. Even so, my simple, rote prayer had all the basic elements of a powerful, effective prayer.

It was heartfelt. "Lord, I offer up my prayer for my husband. I desire his salvation, that he might know peace with you."

It was directed to God the Father. Jesus told his disciples, "When you pray, say: 'Father ...'" (Luke 11:2).

It was based on biblical principles. God does not want "anyone to perish, but everyone to come to repentance" (2 Peter 3:9).

God hears the prayers of his children, whether eloquent or not. He doesn't require a degree in theology or an understanding of Hebrew or Greek, only that we believe that he loves to hear his children ask. That doesn't mean every prayer is answered the way we want or when we want it. It means that his love for us, the intimate love of a Father for his child, and his desire to hear our requests are what make our prayers powerful and effective.

Father,
I don't know how to pray . . .
Except to pour out my heart to you.
I don't know how to approach you . . .
Except to call you "Father."
I don't even know the proper words . . .
Except that I so want my husband to be saved.
As I grow in my faith, I know my prayers will grow too,
That your Holy Spirit will teach me,
That your Son will intercede on my behalf,
And that you will be delighted just to hear me pray.
So, Lord, hear my prayer!
Amen.

PERSEVERING
PRAYER

❧

Ask and it will be given to you;
seek and you will find; knock and
the door will be opened to you.

LUKE 11:9

❧

My soul is in anguish. How long, O LORD, how long?" cries King David in Psalm 6. His prayer was intense. He wanted God to rescue him, deliver him, answer his prayer.

Maybe your soul isn't in anguish, but it may be discouraged. God isn't answering your prayers, or so it seems to you. You wonder why you even bother to pray at all. Besides, if God is all-powerful, why does he even need our prayers? It's not like we can twist his arm or get him to change his mind.

So, why even pray?

In *Caught in the Middle,* authors Beverly Bush Smith and Patricia DeVorss write, "There are a number of ways we grow when we persist in prayer even though we see no progress."

According to Smith and DeVorss, as we pray for our husbands, we:

- Gain glimmers of God's perspective on our problems and learn to believe in his wisdom, love, and power.
- Gain the courage to persevere in spite of apparent refusal by God.
- Come face to face with our own helplessness and see that we cannot answer our own prayers.

- Deal with our own selfish desires and learn to align our will with God's.
- Grow in trust that God is doing something beautiful in our lives.

How long, O LORD, how long? How long do we keep praying? The answer is clear: As long as it takes for God to be glorified and his will to be accomplished in our lives.

Lord,
Sometimes I don't even understand prayer,
Why you answer some prayers and not others,
Why you sometimes seem silent
When I pray and pray and pray . . .
And see nothing change.
Yet, you say to keep asking, keep seeking, keep knocking.
But it's hard, Lord. So hard to keep at it.
Still, I know that "perseverance must finish its work"
So that I may be "mature and complete, not lacking anything"
    (James 1:4).
I know that perseverance produces character
And character produces hope . . . and hope does not disappoint
    (Romans 5:4–5).
I also know that you will not disappoint,
So I will continue praying
No matter how long it takes.
Amen.

GOD'S WORD,
MY PRAYERS

*May the words of my mouth
and the meditation of my heart
be pleasing in your sight, O LORD,
my Rock and my Redeemer.*

PSALM 19:14

S ometimes I don't know how to pray. I want to pray effectively; I want to pray prayers that avail much and make a difference. I want my prayers to work—in my life, in my husband's life.

In their book *Praying the Bible for Your Marriage,* David and Heather Kopp write about the tremendous power in praying God's Word—what they call "praying the Bible back to God"—by taking a passage of Scripture, personalizing it, and then applying it to one's own heart's needs.

According to the Kopps, using the Bible as the basis of our prayers accomplishes several things. Praying God's Word:

- Reminds us of God's promises.
- Helps us avoid the trap of rote praying.
- Shifts the focus of our prayer from our human needs and feelings to God's character, his promises, his past faithfulness, and his goodness.
- Changes us.
- Assures us that our prayers lie within and affirm God's will.

One of my favorite Scriptures to pray for my husband is Isaiah 30:21: "Whether you turn to the right or to the left, your ears will hear a voice behind you, saying, 'This is the way; walk in it.'"

Another one is Isaiah 65:1: "I revealed myself to those who did not ask for me; I was found by those who did not seek me."

Praying the Bible opens our hearts to allow the Holy Spirit to minister to us, and it's Scripture that leads us into an encounter with the Father-heart of God.

> *Faithful God,*
> *Your Word is a lamp to my feet*
> *And a light to my path.*
> *It comforts me, teaches me, guides me.*
> *By using your Word in my prayers,*
> *I'm reminded of your faithfulness throughout all generations.*
> *Your Word contains promises I can hold on to,*
> *And it reveals your heart*
> *For me,*
> *For my husband,*
> *For my marriage.*
> *Like the psalmist, I also pray,*
> *"Remember your word to your servant, for you have given*
> *   me hope" (Psalm 119:49).*
> *Amen.*

DON'T
GIVE UP!

Let us not become weary in doing good, for at the proper time we will reap a harvest if we do not give up.

GALATIANS 6:9

I n my years as a religion reporter, I've often gone into interviews "cold." I have no idea who the person is or where the interview will lead. But God always knows.

I recall one memorable pastor who revealed how, when he was dating his now-wife, he pretended to be a Christian in order to get his (Christian) girlfriend to marry him. Then shortly after they married, he stopped pretending and quit going to church altogether.

He told her she could "take care of the religion" in the family. *Real men didn't need Jesus,* or so he thought. It took him seventeen years before he realized that real men do, indeed, need Jesus.

The one thing this man admired most about his wife during that time was the way she stayed faithful to the Lord and faithful to the church, despite his lack of involvement and her disappointment and sense of betrayal. Even when he needed their only car to go to work on Sunday mornings, she would get their two sons up and dressed and would walk to the nearest church.

As the pastor talked, he looked directly into my eyes. "She didn't give up; she wouldn't give up," he said. Those were the exact words I needed to hear at that moment. His wife didn't give up hoping and praying, doing what's right and trusting God. As a result, at the proper time she reaped a harvest, and her husband is now a pastor.

That's no guarantee that your husband or my husband will become pastors, only that we will reap a harvest of blessings from God's hand—if we don't give up.

Lord of the harvest,
Thank you for the stories you send me of other women
Who didn't, who don't, who won't give up.
Stories of your faithfulness
In times of trouble and stress and disappointment.
Whenever I hear such testimonies, my faith is boosted.
Because they kept going,
Because you kept them going,
I can continue praying . . . and hoping.
I can go on . . . alone in my faith,
Yet not alone, for you are with me.
It's worth the wait to keep going,
To keep doing.
A harvest is coming if I don't give up—
And I don't want to miss it.
Amen.

HOPE DEFERRED . . .
AND RENEWED

---·ᵉᵖ·---

Hope deferred makes the heart sick,
but a longing fulfilled is a tree of life.

PROVERBS 13:12

---·ᵉᵖ·---

What is it that you hope for? If you're reading this book, my guess is that you hope your husband will come to faith in Christ—soon. You hope he will be excited to grow in grace, that he will hunger and thirst for righteousness, that he will hunger and thirst for you.

You hope the two of you will serve the Lord together. Maybe you once did, but now he's fallen away. You hope you'll pray together one day, join a small group or Bible study, stay up late at night discussing your mutual faith.

You hope . . . and you hope . . . and you hope.

You pray and you wait, for months, for years, for decades. Then one day you find yourself heartsick. There's no other word to describe it. Hope deferred and kept out of your reach finally takes its toll on you.

My situation is never going to change, you tell yourself. *Hoping just leads to disappointment, and I'm tired of being disappointed. God has forgotten me.*

The psalmist poured out the agony in his own downcast soul in Psalm 42. He, too, was heartsick. But instead of giving up and giving in, he instructed his heart to "put your hope in

God" (v. 5). Not hope in circumstances changing or in life being different, but hope in God—his glory, his character, his loving care, and his faithfulness to his children.

My heart becomes sick when my hope is misplaced. But when I put my hope in God alone, my heart is renewed and my longing fulfilled.

Lord,
It's a fine line
Between desiring and praying for my husband's salvation
And placing my whole hope in it.
I hope all these things will happen,
But the object and focus of my hope is you.
You alone revive my spirit.
You alone renew my strength.
You alone are my source of life, of love, of peace—
Of hope itself.
"Why are you downcast, O my soul?" the psalmist asked.
"Why so disturbed within me?
Put your hope in God,
For I will yet praise him,
my Savior and my God."
Amen.

THE STORM
BEFORE THE CALM

---

*He got up, rebuked the wind
and said to the waves, "Quiet!
Be still!" Then the wind died down
and it was completely calm.*

MARK 4:39

In the gospel of Mark, Jesus directed his disciples to get into a boat and row to the other side of the lake. As he slept, a "furious squall" came up, a sudden, violent storm that rocked the disciples' boat. They were terrified and accused Jesus of not caring about their desperate predicament.

"Teacher, don't you care if we drown?" they demanded.

He got up, rebuked the wind, and stilled the storm with a simple command. "Quiet! Be still!"

Have you been in that boat lately? Maybe tension between you and your husband is at its highest. Maybe you're discouraged. God seems distant; your husband is distant too.

Or maybe you're fighting. Your husband seems to delight in provoking you, taunting you, making fun of your faith. Maybe things are worse between you than you ever dared to imagine. Only God can fix things. Only he can still the storm that's ravaging your home—but he's asleep. Not really, but to you it feels as if he is.

He's asleep, and you're scared. You don't know where to turn. So you do the only thing you know to do. You cry out, "Lord, don't you care? Lord, do something!"

It could be that the storm rages even stronger . . . for a little while longer.

Then, as you're bailing water out of your boat, as you're crying with exhaustion and near despair, with a simple, authoritative word, God arises and brings calm.

Afterward, he tells you that he was there with you all the time and he wasn't about to let you drown. He reminds you that the wind and the waves, and even your husband, your in-laws, your finances, your kids, and everything that concerns you, are all subject to his command.

After all, he's God.

God, whom even the wind and the waves obey.

Sovereign God,
You are Lord of my storms as well as God of my calm.
You are with me no matter what,
And you are always in complete control,
Even when everything around me seems out of control,
I know I shouldn't fear;
I know I shouldn't fret and worry and cry,
Yet I do—and I even blame you.
"Don't you even care?" I accuse.
Forgive me, Lord, for I know you do.
When I'm afraid, I tend to forget.
But you've never let me down.
You always still the storm,
Even if it's only the storm within my restless heart.
I praise you, my Lord and my Rock,
My Anchor and my God.
Amen.

WHEN MONEY DIVIDES

─────────────── ⁊ℰ ───────────────

Each . . . should give what he has
decided in his heart to give.

2 CORINTHIANS 9:7

─────────────── ⁊ℰ ───────────────

I love to tell this story. I had only been a Christian a few months, and my husband didn't have a problem with me putting a "reasonable" amount in the offering plate at church. But as far as he was concerned, a tithe of ten percent was not reasonable, and I didn't push the issue.

At the time, I didn't have any income of my own, but I wanted to give Jesus a birthday offering at Christmas. So, I told God that if I received any money in my name by the time my own birthday arrived (December 10), I wanted to give it all to Jesus for his birthday on Christmas.

I shouldn't have been surprised, though I was, as money started pouring in from everywhere in answer to my prayer. By my birthday, I had fifty dollars. I also had a pile of bills that needed paying and a husband who didn't understand how I could give money to the church when we needed it.

I told him, "I don't know how, but I know God will bless us if we give this money to him."

That was too much for him to take. He had been working twelve-hour days and his Jesus-freak wife had flipped out. He stormed off to work on the morning of my birthday, so angry that I wasn't sure if he would even come home.

But he did, and God did, indeed, bless my fifty dollars. By the time Barry came home from work I had received $150 more in that day's mail. I was able to give the fifty dollars as an offering, plus we had three times that much to pay bills.

In marriage, money is one of the great dividers. However, "God is able to make all grace abound to you, so that in all things at all times, having all that you need, you will abound in every good work" (2 Corinthians 9:8).

You can take that to the bank.

Heavenly Father,
You who own the cattle on a thousand hills,
Who own everything and have need of nothing,
You are more than able to enable me to give.
My heart,
So filled with gratitude for all you've done for me,
Desires to worship you
With my money as well as my praise.
But it's difficult, Lord, when my husband doesn't understand.
I know I'm to be submissive to him,
But I also want to give to you.
Since you put that desire within me,
I know that you can and will fulfill it.
So, I'll wait expectantly to see how you're going to do it.
I can't wait to be amazed!
Amen.

CREATING A
LIFE PRAYER

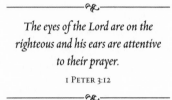

*The eyes of the Lord are on the
righteous and his ears are attentive
to their prayer.*

1 PETER 3:12

Several years ago a little book called *The Prayer of Jabez* swept through the Christian world. Its author, Bruce Wilkinson, took a two-sentence prayer found in 1 Chronicles 4 and made it his life's prayer. Although I'm cautious about rote recitation in prayer, there's something to be said about having a definite focus.

Karen, a woman in my Moms In Touch prayer group, told me of another woman who lamented that her prayers for her husband were random and sporadic. He spent long hours in his workshop apart from the family. Concerned about how this was affecting the family, she began to pray:

"Lord, put your arm around his shoulder. Whisper your secret in his ear. Fill his heart with your love and bring him to the fulfillment of your purpose for his life here on earth. Amen."

After a time of regularly praying this prayer, God graciously moved in her husband's life. Later he told her, "It was as if the Lord put his hand on my shoulder and spoke in my ear about his love for me and what my purpose is here on earth."

I got goose bumps as Karen told me that story. Isn't God awesome? He puts the prayer in our hearts to pray, and then he answers it, while we stand amazed.

How comforting, how exciting to know that when it comes to prayer, whether we pray with our own words or with his, the Lord listens . . . and he answers.

Lord,
You are well acquainted with my desires for my husband.
You know what he needs
And how my heart aches for him to know you.
This is my prayer for him:
Open his eyes to the full weight of his sin,
Yet at the same time
May he see the full measure of your mercy and grace.
Keep him from evil
And let him know how much you long to smile on him.
This is my prayer for myself:
Strengthen me, guide me, teach me to pray.
Encourage me and cover me with your love.
Keep me from evil, too,
For I love you, Lord.
Amen.

THE PRESSURE
TO BE PERFECT

---

*Therefore, there is now no
condemnation for those who are in
Christ Jesus, because through Christ
Jesus the law of the Spirit of life set me
free from the law of sin and death.*

ROMANS 8:1–2

I thought you said you were a Christian.

Have you heard that before? You've yelled at the kids, you got caught telling a lie, or your husband overheard you gossiping. Even though you try as hard as you can to maintain a Christian witness that your husband might see how knowing Christ has changed you, you keep blowing it, and he keeps seeing it. Not only that, but he seems to find great pleasure in pointing it out to you.

You feel terrible. You think you've let God down. You berate yourself. *My husband will never see Christ in me now! I've lost credibility. He's right—I am a hypocrite.*

You want so badly to show your husband what new life in Christ means. You don't want to be a stumbling block to his coming to faith, so you vow to do better. Try harder.

But that's not the gospel. That's not true Christianity. The gospel is that we're saved by grace and we live by grace. Yes, we're progressively getting better, but it's the Spirit working from within who changes us and not we who change ourselves by our own efforts.

To be a genuine example of what a Christian is, let your husband see you struggle and fall. (He sees it anyway.) Let him see that the Christian life is one of repentance and process. Then when your husband says, "I thought you were a Christian," you can tell him that you are.

Being a Christian doesn't mean you're perfect. It means sometimes you take two steps forward and one step back; sometimes you take five steps back. But God loves you anyway, just because you're his.

God of grace,
You have set me free to obey you,
To walk with you, and to be your child.
You're changing me every day.
How I marvel at all you're doing in me!
But . . .
I'm not what I should be nor what I could be,
And that seems to be the only thing my husband ever sees.
He thinks Christians should be "perfect,"
But only Christ is perfect, exchanging his perfection for my sin.
Although you've given me a new nature
With the desire not to sin—
And the ability to say no to sin—
I have such a long way to go; I'm still a work in progress.
Ah, but you have set me free! No condemnation!
You haven't called me to be anything more than real.
Help me to rest in that truth,
That my husband may see and know that indeed,
I am a Christian.
Amen.

WHY DOES
DADDY . . . ?

---

*The man without the Spirit
does not accept the things that come
from the Spirit of God, for they
are foolishness to him, and he cannot
understand them because they
are spiritually discerned.*

1 CORINTHIANS 2:14

Why does Daddy always drink beer? Why does Daddy say bad words? Why doesn't Daddy go to church with us?

How do you answer these questions honestly without showing disrespect to your husband's position as head of the family?

In his book *Unbelieving Husbands and the Wives Who Love Them*, Michael Fanstone writes, "When problems in the family are largely over your personal faith that your husband does not share, explain this to the children with tact and sensitivity. . . . You can then explain that their dad does not feel the same way about God."

Beware of the temptation to create an "us against Dad" conspiracy. When it comes to explaining the spiritual differences between Daddy and the rest of the family, keep it matter of fact and judgment-free. Try something like this:

"Not everybody believes in Jesus, and it's Jesus who helps us not to use bad language or drink too much beer. Jesus helps us want to go to church. Right now Daddy doesn't know that, but that doesn't mean he's a bad person."

With older children, explain that a person without Christ can't be expected to act like a Christian because it's only the Holy Spirit in us who is good and who enables us to be good.

No matter what the age of your children, it's important to demonstrate an honest and genuine love and respect for their father. Kids can spot phoniness blindfolded. It's a balancing act to be able to know exactly how to answer a child's questions, but God will give you the right words to say as you trust in him.

Lord,
Once I was in darkness, too,
Before you rescued me.
When I keep that in mind,
It's easier not to be judgmental toward my husband.
(Although you know sometimes I am.)
Still, it's hard to know what to say to the kids.
"Love the sinner, hate the sin," sounds good in theory
But when my kids are affected,
When they are confused and hurting . . .
Lord,
I know I can't expect Christlike behavior
From a man who's without Christ.
But my kids . . .
Please give us all the grace we need
To love him as he is and for who he is—
He's ours, and I am yours.
Amen.

"STICKS AND STONES"

She brings him good, not harm,
all the days of her life.

PROVERBS 31:12

I f you gathered a handful of your closest friends and asked them to describe your husband based solely on the things you say about him, what would they say?

If your husband overheard you talking to your friends about him, would you be comfortable? Or would you be ashamed?

Oh, how we women love to talk! God wired us with a need to talk things out with one another. It's how we relieve stress and gain perspective. However, there's a fine line separating "confiding" from "gossiping." I may be careful at home and guard my words *to* my husband, but I can still wound him by what I say *about* him to others.

I will never forget overhearing my former pastor's wife saying, "From what some women tell me about their husbands, by the time I meet the guys, I already hate them."

For me, that was a pivotal, eye-opening moment. Although I wasn't part of her conversation, her words could've been directed toward me. Like a slap in the face, her words shocked me. I had been guilty of tearing down my husband with my words, and I knew it.

Immediately, I repented. I didn't want my pastor's wife or anybody else to hate my husband based on what I said about him. I vowed never to say anything to dishonor him ever again. Of course, a vow like that is hard to keep, but God had begun a wonderful work of grace in my heart that day, changing my words from harmful to helpful.

I want it to be said of me that I bring my husband good, not harm, all the days of my life. He deserves no less.

Father,
Too often I speak without thinking.
I don't mean to harm my husband,
But that's what I end up doing.
Even when I think what I'm saying is okay,
"Sharing my heart,"
If it tears down the one you gave me to love,
If it makes other people think badly of him,
Then it's not okay.
It's harmful. It's wrong. It's sin.
I repent, Lord!
Change my heart, curb my tongue,
That the words of my mouth
And the meditations of my heart
May be acceptable to you and helpful to my husband—
That I may do him good, not harm,
All the days of my life, and of his.
Amen.

THE MAN IN
THE MIRROR

---

*"In this world you will have
trouble. But take heart!
I have overcome the world."*

JOHN 16:33

Former atheist Lee Strobel recalls his jumble of emotions that
followed his wife's conversion to Christianity. In *Surviving a
Spiritual Mismatch in Marriage* he writes about his resentment
and jealousy, his frustration, fear, and suspicion. He hated thinking that his children would grow up to pity him or think of him
as a "hell-bound reprobate." Even though his wife was careful
not to criticize, he felt she didn't approve of his friends, his foul
language, and especially his drinking binges.

He recalls an ever-present, seething anger that would often
erupt in fits of shouting; once he kicked a hole in the living
room wall. Afterward, he says his wife stood there speechless,
their daughter started to cry, and immediately he "felt like a
jerk."

Although back then he didn't understand what was going
on to cause such rage, today he offers this insight: "The more
Leslie opened her life to Christ and pursued a God-honoring
way of life, the more her behavior had the effect of unmasking
the ugliness, selfishness, and immorality of my own lifestyle."

He says his wife, Leslie, didn't have to confront or lecture
him. "Merely living out her Christian life in my presence was

like holding up a mirror to me." He adds, "For the first time, I was seeing myself as I really was—*and I didn't like the picture!*"

Strobel says an unbelieving husband's anger can be frightening, his silent treatments can be disconcerting, his sulking can be childish, and his resentments unfair—but they just might be signs that God is at work.

And that's good news.

So if this describes your home life right now, sit back, take heart, and hang on tight.

Lord,
You have a way of shaking things up.
You enter our status quo
And disrupt everything.
You change a woman,
Give her new desires for purity and godliness,
Give her a joy and a peace that she can't explain,
And send her home to her
      bewildered/resentful/jealous/fearful/angry husband.
For my own husband,
As he looks in the mirror,
As he's confronted with his sin,
And lashes out in anger at what he sees,
Give me patience, give me grace, give me peace.
Help me to see beyond his outbursts to the truth
That you are at work in his life,
And also in mine.
In your name, I pray.
Amen.

WHO'S
THE BOSS?

---
*... the unfading beauty of a gentle
and quiet spirit, which is of
great worth in God's sight.*

I PETER 3:4

One day as my husband and I good-naturedly sparred over "who's the boss" in our relationship, he said that, of course, he was.

"No, I just let you think you are," I told him.

He laughed. "No, I'm the boss," he replied.

"See how good I am?" I said. "You actually think you're the boss!" With that, I rendered him speechless.

Spouses sparring over "who's the boss" has been going on for millennia. Back in the Garden of Eden, after the Fall, God told Eve, "Your desire will be for your husband, and he will rule over you" (Genesis 3:16). Some biblical scholars define that word "desire" as a physical, sexual, and emotional longing a wife will have for her husband. Other theologians offer another meaning: A woman will desire to usurp her husband's role as head of the family. She will constantly battle with him and within herself over who's in charge.

As women, we hold tremendous power in a relationship. It's said, "The hand that rocks the cradle rules the world." We often set the tone in a marriage. The question is, what tone do we want to set?

In God's design of marriage, he has set the husband as the head and calls the wife to follow, to adapt, to arrange herself under. True submission in marriage is not subservience. It's not subjecting oneself to abuse or mistreatment, nor is it going along with sin. Neither does it mean not having an opinion or input.

Instead, it's a voluntary yielding to another, a wife's deferring to her husband and not demanding her own way. It means allowing a man and empowering him to make the final decisions in your family, unless that means violating Scripture.

When a woman chooses not to exert her power, when she lays aside her sense of entitlement and reigns in her desire to have her own way, it demonstrates the character of Christ to her unbelieving husband. And when it's done with genuine gentleness and quietness of spirit, as an act of worship unto the Lord, God is, indeed, pleased, and the woman is blessed.

Lord,
It's a constant battle, isn't it? This struggle to be the boss.
I want to be in charge! I want to call the shots!
But whenever I do get my own way,
I may be happy for a moment, but it's an empty victory
Because my husband is demoralized, and you, my Lord, are
*   dishonored.*
You say the husband is to be head over the wife.
It's your design for my life, for my marriage and my home.
Even if my husband doesn't obey the Word,
By my obeying you,
Yielding control and submitting from my heart
—Just as Jesus did—
Life is much more peaceful, and you, Lord, are pleased.
Change my heart, I pray!
Make me more like Jesus.
Amen.

TURN YOUR EYES UPON JESUS

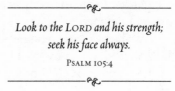

Look to the LORD and his strength;
seek his face always.

PSALM 105:4

It didn't take long for me to diagnose Sherry's vision problems. I'd seen the symptoms many times before, especially in my own life. The only thing Sherry could see was the lack of faith in her unbelieving husband, Brad.

When they had first met and married, Brad had said he loved Jesus. They had gone to church together, prayed together. But after a few years Brad stopped praying with Sherry and then stopped going to church. Now, seven years later, Brad tells Sherry that he doesn't believe God exists. He's angry and belittles Sherry for continuing to believe "that crock."

Understandably, Sherry is devastated. However, instead of turning her eyes toward God and allowing him to help her deal with her marriage as it is now, for the past several years Sherry has kept her eyes focused on Brad's spiritual condition, asking him regularly, "Were you ever a believer?"

This makes Brad even angrier. Sherry's tunnel vision is driving a wedge between them—and she can't see it.

We all have vision problems at times. It doesn't mean we're bad; it just means we're human, and we hurt. It's part of human nature to focus on the other guy.

Because word pictures are so powerful, I told Sherry to think of an overweight woman whose husband monitors every bite of food she eats. He may be genuinely concerned for his wife's health and well-being, but his continual focus on her weight doesn't help her. Instead, she feels demoralized, judged, and condemned.

In Sherry's case, whether Brad ever believed or not is moot; he says he doesn't now, and hounding him about it does neither of them any good. Nobody was ever nagged into the kingdom of God.

Thankfully, this story has a happy ending. Once Sherry corrected her vision problem, the tension in her marriage began to lessen. Brad still claims God doesn't exist, but because Sherry isn't focused on his spiritual condition, she's able to see that even in this, God can and will sustain her. And Brad has seemed to be less antagonistic as time goes on.

We are called to be ministers of reconciliation, channels of grace, and we can only do that when we turn our eyes upon Jesus.

My precious Jesus,
Once again I come to you
Aware of my weakness, aware of my sin—
Watching my husband in judgment, not looking to you for
*   strength and hope and peace.*
Oh, how my soul longs for peace!
It's only when I turn my eyes upon you that I find it.
Just as the hymn says, "The things of earth will grow strangely
*   dim*
In the light of (your) glory and grace."
Lord, lift my head and open my eyes,
That I may see you.
That I may find life more abundant and free!
Amen.

CONTENTMENT
OF DESIRE

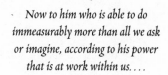

I n the quietness of your dreams, when you dare to desire, what is it that you imagine? What is it that you long for concerning your husband, your family, your marriage? Do you long for your husband to share your faith in Christ? Of course you do. But . . .

But you dare not desire too often or too deeply. You bury your desire in case it never comes to pass. That way, you can protect your heart from the grief of disappointment. But . . .

But desire keeps pushing to the forefront, and you scold yourself for it. You tell your soul, "Be quiet!" You tell your soul to wait patiently, and you feel guilty for your desire.

In *The Journey of Desire,* John Eldredge writes, "Paul said he had learned the secret of being content (Philippians 4:12), and many Christians assume he no longer experienced the thirst of his soul. . . . [However] contentment is not freedom *from* desire, but freedom *of* desire. Being content is not pretending that everything is the way you wish it would be; it is not acting as though you have no wishes. Rather, it is no longer being *ruled* by your desires."

Desiring to see your husband come to faith in Christ is a good desire, a God-given desire. Contentment doesn't change that. Contentment is daring to continue dreaming and longing, yet leaving the outcome to the One who is able to grant you the deepest desires of your heart . . . and even more.

Father,
Your Word says that you satisfy the desires of every living thing,
And you do satisfy me—
You fill my longings, bring me joy, fill me with peace.
But . . .
There's a desire within me that remains unsatisfied,
A longing to see my husband find saving faith in you.
I wrestle with knowing that you want me to be content
And this desire that I believe you put within me.
Help me to rest in contentment,
Content that you are able to fulfill my deep desires;
Content that you are God
And that you are able to do immeasurably more.
For your glory, I pray.
Amen.

ROOTS OF REJECTION

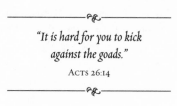

*"It is hard for you to kick
against the goads."*

ACTS 26:14

H er name is Katie. She called late one night, crying. She and her husband had just had a terrible fight. He stormed out, but not before telling her that he never wanted to hear the name Jesus, didn't ever want to see anyone from the church, didn't even want her to pray for him.

She told me that when they married five years before, Jerry had been a strong Christian. Up until six months ago, they prayed together, worshiped together, even did street ministry together.

Then Jerry started drifting from his faith. He had taken a second job on Sundays and stopped going to church. Then he stopped praying with her. "Lately," she said, "he can't even stand to be in the same room with me."

They hadn't made love in more than three months.

The one thread of hope Katie clung to as she told me her story was Jerry's words as he stormed out the door: "When I look at you, I see God, and right now I don't want to deal with him, so I can't deal with you either."

Even though she felt personally rejected by her husband, she knew he was really rejecting God. "As painful as this is, at the same time it shows me that God is at work," she said. "That's why Jerry's kicking. It's the Lord he's fighting, not me."

Jesus told his disciples that when they were insulted, rejected, and persecuted because of him, to rejoice and be glad, for great would be their reward. He didn't say it would be easy or without pain, but he did say they would be blessed.

If you are feeling the pain of rejection because of your faith in Christ, keep in mind that you are not alone. Jesus, the One who was also rejected, promises to never leave you nor forsake you.

So, run to him with your hurt and rejection . . . and be blessed.

Precious Jesus,
They persecuted and rejected you;
They spit in your face
And falsely accused you.
You promised that that would happen to me too;
People would hate me because they hate you more.
But Lord,
When that rejection comes from the one I love . . .
Oh, how it hurts!
I offer you this pain I feel to use for your glory.
Thank you for the comfort of your Holy Spirit;
Thank you for your sufficient grace.
Thank you that you consider me worthy to be rejected for
*   your name's sake.*
Even though I hurt right now,
I know that I am blessed.
Amen.

RECIPE FOR A
GRACE SANDWICH

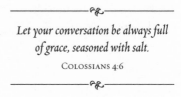

*Let your conversation be always full
of grace, seasoned with salt.*

COLOSSIANS 4:6

How are you at confrontation? Do you avoid bringing up anything that might lead to conflict? Or is your style "in your face"?

When it comes to marital relationships, even in the best ones, partners need occasionally to confront one another, and it's rarely easy. When it involves confronting an unbelieving husband, there's an added difficulty. *If I say something, will he perceive it as an attempt to "convert" him? Will he accuse me of being "holier than thou"? Should I remain silent and just let God convict him?*

Consider learning to make grace sandwiches.

Bill Hybels writes in *Honest to God,* "Don't put up your dukes and start throwing punches. . . . Affirm the relationship before you open up the agenda. Say, 'Look honey, I love you and value our relationship. I want our marriage to be all it can be, and I believe it has the potential to be mutually satisfying in every way. But I need to talk to you about a few things that are standing in the way."

Then you deliver your message by pointing out the behavior and not attacking his character. ("I think you have a drinking problem," not "You're a lousy drunk.") Finally, you end with more affirmation. ("I love you and am committed to you.")

This doesn't guarantee that your husband will accept your message, but that's not your responsibility. You are responsible to serve him a meal, sandwiched by grace.

Chances are he'll be hungry for it.

Father,
You always deliver your messages to me
Wrapped in grace.
You point out my sin without condemning my person.
When you correct,
I'm never demeaned.
"You told a lie," not "You're a stinking liar."
Teach me, Lord, your ways of grace!
That my words to my husband—
Even those hard words of correction—
May be accepted in the spirit in which they're given . . .
In love.
Oh, may I have a heart that loves!
In Jesus' name.
Amen.

JESUS, I AM RESTING, RESTING

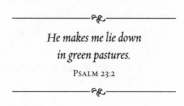

He makes me lie down
in green pastures.

PSALM 23:2

Whenever I meet a woman who is married to an unbelieving husband, one of her first questions is, "What can I *do*?" Next she'll launch into all the ways she has tried to get her husband to go to church, read a Christian book, attend a Christian conference. She'll fret and wring her hands and ask me to please pray for him and their marriage.

When she finally comes up for air, I'll tell her my best answer for what she should do: Relax. Stop your fretting and rest.

Then she'll say, "Yeah, but . . ."

In God's kingdom, there is no such thing as "Yeah, but." He bids us rest in him. He knows a husband's needs and he knows what it takes to turn his attention toward him. He doesn't need our fussing and fretting and our frantic efforts to do his work for him.

Yes, we're to pray and to be ministers of reconciliation and grace and serve with gentle submission, but primarily we're to rest.

"Resting in the Lord does not depend on external circumstances at all, but on your relationship to God Himself," writes

Oswald Chambers in *My Utmost for His Highest*. "Fussing always ends in sin. We imagine that a little anxiety and worry are an indication of how really wise we are; it is much more an indication of how really wicked we are. Fretting springs from a determination to get our own way."

When I'm convinced that God knows what he's doing and that his way is better than mine, I can rest—

Rest in what he's going to do. Rest in what he's already done. Rest in who he is.

He is God.

Jesus,
You inspired the hymn writer Jean Pigott to write about
    resting, resting—
Resting in you, resting "in the joy of what Thou art."
As I do, I, too, find "out the greatness of Thy loving heart."
You told your fretful disciples that worry never changed a thing.
You told them to come to you for rest;
You say the same thing to me.
Although my sin nature wants to fret and worry and do, do, do.
Yet, when I'm "resting 'neath Thy smile, Lord Jesus,"
When I relax and trust that you are working,
In my life and in my husband's,
Earth's dark shadows do, indeed, flee.
Hallelujah!
May I continually take my rest in you.
Amen.

LIVING IN THE NOW

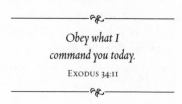

*Obey what I
command you today.*

EXODUS 34:11

It's been said that today is all we have. Yesterday is gone and tomorrow hasn't yet arrived. *Today,* I am called to love my husband and serve my family, not as they were *yesterday* or as they might or might not be *tomorrow,* but as they are *today.*

For women married to unbelieving husbands, it's tempting to put today on hold. *Today he makes fun of my faith; today he's antagonistic; today I'm lonely and frustrated.*

Today I just want to think about tomorrow.

There's nothing wrong with thinking about tomorrow and the hope of God answering our prayers for the salvation of a mate. The danger lies in living solely for tomorrow to the exclusion of today.

I knew a woman whose entire life revolved around "next Christmas." I don't think she ever experienced a May 5 or an October 23 or even a "this" Christmas. Because all her thoughts and energy were in the future, she never seemed to live in the present.

A woman in an unequally yoked marriage often does this too. She looks at her husband and thinks, *I will love you so much . . . I will be such a good wife . . . we will be so happy, once you accept Christ.*

She holds back from giving her whole heart until tomorrow. It's subtle and often subconscious, but her husband gets the message: "*Today* you don't love me." If there are too many todays like that, he might not stay around for tomorrow.

Even if your marriage isn't what you hope it would be today, today is what you have been given. So, live in the now. Accept your relationship for what it is. Go ahead and hope for tomorrow, but focus on today. Ask yourself, "What's good about today? What can I do to make it better?" Then ask God to help you do it.

Lord,
Sometimes today is hard.
I've changed. I'm not who I was yesterday . . .
But he is, and he's not who I want him to be.
It's painful to say that, but it's how I feel.
I'm confessing it now to you as the sin that it is.
I lift up our marriage to you today.
Someday I hope it will be different.
Someday I hope we will both love and serve you. Together.
But today . . .
You've given me today to do what you've called me to do:
Love my husband as he is today—
Without thoughts of what he could be like tomorrow.
Tomorrow may be a long way off.
But today is here.
And today is all I have.
Lord, may you be glorified in my life today.
Amen.

LISTENING WITH LOVE

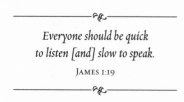

Everyone should be quick
to listen [and] slow to speak.

JAMES 1:19

One of the biggest complaints men have about women is our propensity for talking too much. Men want "just the facts, ma'am." We lose them with our attention to every detail and nuance as we attempt to get our stories out.

When it comes to communicating the message of the gospel to an unbelieving husband, I want my words to count. But if I'm in the habit of blabbering everything that's on my mind and my husband is in the habit of tuning me out, then when there is an open door to speak, I risk having my words go unheard.

Being a newspaper reporter has given me years of listening practice. In order to get someone's story correct, I need to devote myself to paying attention and trying to understand the meaning behind a person's words. In the course of an interview I ask follow-up questions for clarification. I dig deeper. I want to know what the person has to say. Often when I finish an interview, the person thanks me for letting him or her speak. I've learned that it's all about the other person; it's not about me.

I've tried to bring this skill home. I still talk too much—that's what we women do—but I have become a better listener. And because I listen first, my husband seems more open when I speak.

Listening with love is one of the greatest ways a wife can show honor to her husband. Even if his beliefs are contrary to the Word of God, he is still a person who longs to be heard.

To listen with love:

- Maintain eye contact.
- Don't interrupt.
- Ask questions.
- Listen intentionally and actively.
- If you don't understand something being said, don't assume meaning—ask.
- Be patient.

Lord,
You are the perfect example
Of how to listen with love.
You didn't bombard the woman at the well
With a three-point sermon
Or a rapid-fire string of rules and regulations.
Instead, you drew her out,
Met her at her felt need,
Listened to her speak.
Help me, Lord,
To be quicker to listen than to speak;
To love as you loved—
With my ears as well as with my mouth
And always with my heart.
Amen.

LIGHTING A FIRE
WITH YOUR WORDS

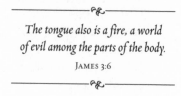

*The tongue also is a fire, a world
of evil among the parts of the body.*

JAMES 3:6

D o you recall the old camp song, "It Only Takes a Spark to Get a Fire Going?" Although that song is about spreading the fire of the gospel, it also describes the destructive power of our words that can destroy like a wildfire in the brush.

What wife doesn't know her husband's hot buttons? Add to the usual, everyday opportunities for conflict the particular tensions that accompany a spiritually unequal marriage, and you have a potential fire hazard.

Clifford Notarius calls certain words "expressions of hot thoughts" that "spur the body to prepare for an all-out fight, making it difficult to have a conversation." Other words are warm, making conversation as inviting as a campfire on a cold night.

Wildfire words include:

You never _____.
I hate _____.
Why can't you ever_____?
You heathen!
You're a jerk.
Your friends are jerks.

If you were a Christian _____.
You're going to hell.
I can't take this anymore.

Campfire words include:
I understand.
What can I do for you?
I'm sorry.
Tell me your dreams.
I need you.
Will you help me?
I admire you because _____.
You're doing a good job.
I appreciate the way you _____.
I love you.

Lord,
One word, just one word can burn like a forest on fire.
One word can turn harmony to turmoil,
Demolish a home,
Destroy a life.
One word, just one word can also warm a heart,
Turn turmoil to harmony,
Restore a home,
Bring healing to a life.
Oh, how I regret the wildfires I've set with my words!
Forgive me and help me to think before I speak—
And speak only words that warm.
May my words be always pleasing to you, Lord,
And uplifting to my husband.
In Jesus' name, I pray.
Amen.

WHAT SEX MEANS TO A MAN

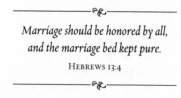

Marriage should be honored by all,
and the marriage bed kept pure.

HEBREWS 13:4

A s women, sex touches the core of who we are; it touches our soul and our spirit. It goes beyond a physical drive. For us, it's an emotional connection, one that most of us don't enter into lightly.

Sex for a man is equally important, but different. As Norm Wright explains in *What Men Want,* men want more from sex than just sex. They want complete and intimate relationships, but often substitute sex for sharing and emotion. Wright says sex is usually a man's only source of closeness.

Tim and Beverly LaHaye say sex fulfills a man's sense of manhood. It makes him a man in his own eyes and gives him self-confidence. It enhances his love for his wife and satisfies his sex drive.

Willard Harley Jr. says sexual fulfillment tops a man's list for needs in a marriage. It's that important to a man.

Although a husband's sexual advances may be physiologically driven, they are most likely the only way he knows how to emotionally connect with his wife. In many cases, the more a Christian wife stays available as a willing responder to her unbelieving husband's sexual advances, or even initiates sexual encounters, the more he will feel appreciated, valued, and loved. The more loved he feels, the more likely he'll be to open his heart to the things his wife cares about.

Maybe even her faith in the Lord.

Gracious Lord,
My husband is not an animal
But a man whom you made,
With drives and needs that I, as a woman,
Often don't understand.
Help me, Lord, to appreciate his needs,
To accommodate his drives,
To enjoy his advances and
To love his embrace.
Lord, give me a willing heart when I'm not in the mood,
That I may be a vessel of your love,
Even in this most intimate way,
To my husband, who so desperately needs your love.
I give you honor in every area of my life.
Amen.

IN THE MOOD?

My lover is mine
and I am his.

SONG OF SONGS 2:16

How's your sexual temperature? A woman once confided that the thought of sex with her non-Christian husband turned her stomach. "He makes fun of my faith; he sits on the couch watching TV all the time; he reeks of beer and isn't involved with anything in my life. Then when it's time for bed, he's all over me. We used to have a great sex life, but not now. Now I just keep busy until he falls asleep, and then I go to bed."

She said she was tired of feeling "used." Reading what the Bible says about a wife's body no longer belonging to herself alone but also to her husband and that spouses are not to deprive each other of sexual availability only made her feel guilty.

"To lie naked next to someone is to allow him or her to know you as no one else does," writes Bob Moeller in *For Better, for Worse, for Keeps*. "So, to reject your husband or wife sexually is to say, as nothing else can say, 'I reject you.'"

When it comes to regaining sexual desire, Moeller suggests using a surefire aphrodisiac—forgiveness. He says forgiveness can dramatically alter the chemistry between two people. "If anger can drive a couple apart, forgiveness can have just the opposite effect. It can be positively magnetic," he writes.

Two other aphrodisiacs Moeller suggests are surrender and unselfishness. When you focus on these and not on your anger and resentment, then God can work to soften your heart and even renew your sexual desire.

After all, sex is his gift to be enjoyed. Talk to him about it.

Father,
Like no other area of my life,
My sexuality reaches to my core.
I want to desire my husband, just as you have designed.
I confess my resentment.
I confess my anger, my self-preservation, and
How I withhold affection sometimes—
Sometimes because he's not a Christian, even though I know
    that's wrong.
Forgiveness doesn't come easily;
I need you to help me, Lord.
You've called me to be my husband's wife,
To serve him in all ways,
Not with gritted teeth or begrudgingly,
But with willingness and vulnerability.
I trust you, Father, to work in my heart,
To rekindle my desire, and to be your instrument of grace.
Amen.

MARRIED FRIENDS

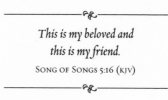

*This is my beloved and
this is my friend.*

SONG OF SONGS 5:16 (KJV)

Do you and your husband have fun together? Often when faith divides a couple, the spiritual tension makes fun difficult. You have your Christian friends; he has his buddies. Unless one or both of you makes an effort, the two of you can easily drift apart until you're nothing more than married roommates.

We were created for connection and, as believers, called to be ministers within marriage. That includes a wife being her husband's friend.

Willard Harley Jr., author of *His Needs, Her Needs,* cites recreational companionship as a man's number two need in marriage, second to sexual fulfillment. A man wants a woman who will share recreational experiences with him.

He wants to have fun.

The more fun you can have together, the closer you'll become. The closer you become, the more relaxed you'll be around each other. When you're relaxed and enjoying each other's company, you're no longer a threat to each other. He stops feeling like you're only out to convert him, and you'll stop seeing him as the enemy.

If it's been awhile since you and your husband have done anything fun together, take heart. Nothing is impossible with God.

Go slow; start small. Ask the Lord to give you nonthreatening ideas for activities the two of you can do together. Here are a few to get you started:

- Go to a high school football or basketball game together.
- Refinish a piece of furniture together.
- Work out together.
- Ask your husband to teach you about his favorite hobby or sport.
- Take photos.
- Volunteer together.
- Visit a museum or flea market.
- Wash your car together.

What else can you think of?

Lord,
Sometimes I feel so distant from my husband
And I can't even imagine us ever being friends.
Things are different now; we're different.
Still, my heart longs for friendship.
I believe that you want that for us too.
You were a friend to everyone, Jesus.
Please create a heart of friendship in me!
Help me to be a friend;
Help me to be a fun person to be around—
Not because I think it will bring my husband closer to faith,
But because it pleases you.
For your honor, I pray.
Amen.

GIVE YOUR
HUSBAND FREEDOM

―――――――――― ❧ ――――――――――

Trust in the LORD *with all*
your heart and lean not on
your own understanding.

PROVERBS 3:5

―――――――――― ❧ ――――――――――

Picture your husband in diapers sitting in a playpen, a pacifier in his mouth. He wants to get out, but you're afraid he'll fall or get lost, so you scold him and tell him you know what's best for him. Then you hand him some gospel tracts, plop him in front of a *Veggie Tales* or *Left Behind* video, and call to arrange a play date for him with the pastor or a deacon from the church.

When you do take your husband out of the playpen and outside to play, you constantly direct his every step and run interference so he won't go the wrong way. *After all, I know what's best,* you think. *I'm only trying to help you in your spiritual walk.*

But your husband doesn't want your help. (If he did, he would ask for it.) Instead, he wants freedom from your hovering over him. He feels emasculated and resentful, and that makes you angry, anxious, and fearful. *What if he never wants to come to church? What if he never opens a Bible? What if he wants to explore a cult religion? What if he falls into sin and it affects me and our children? What if he never finds Christ?*

The truth is, a man will respect a woman who gives him the freedom to be a man, including the freedom to fail or fall. Ironically, the very thing you may be trying to control and keep from happening in your husband's life is the very thing God may want to use to bring him to his knees. Your "helping" just gets in the way.

As women, we mean well. But often our instincts, "leaning on our own understanding," reap results opposite from what we intend. That's why God says to trust him.

The Lord is able. He can direct your husband and catch him if he falls. Allow your husband to be the man God created him to be. Give him the freedom to examine the claims of Christ and respond to the Spirit's drawing for himself. Pray like crazy, put your trust in the Lord, then stand back and see what good things freedom brings.

Faithful Father,
You know my heart—
You know that I only want to help my husband to believe.
But I confess, I'm often blind to the effects of my "helping."
You say to trust you and not to trust in myself.
It's hard, Lord.
Trusting doesn't come easily.
Still, I want to do what's best for my husband,
To do what honors him as a man
And pleases you as my God.
Lord, by faith, I set him free and into your loving hands.
For I know that I can trust you
To do what's best for us both.
Amen.

How Much
Do I Tell?

*The heart of the righteous
weighs its answers.*

PROVERBS 15:28

G od wired women with a need to talk things out. The deeper the pain or the more troubling the situation, the more we need to verbalize it. That's how we sort out our feelings and make sense of our emotions. We think out loud.

However, when it comes to disclosing the details of marital struggles, how much information is too much? Where is the line between gossip and a legitimate need to talk? Should a woman even discuss her marital conflict? Or is that being disrespectful?

Although I haven't always lived up to them, here are the guidelines I use before I talk to anyone about private issues involving my husband:

1. Tell God first. Tell him everything, including all the hateful, revengeful, mean, ugly, nasty, name-calling, blaming garbage.
2. If I still feel the need to talk, go only to my prayer partners and/or pastor, leaving out all the "garbage" I've already left with God. Instead, I stick only to the facts and my feelings—no judgments against my husband (for example, "He's such a jerk!").

3. When acquaintances ask how I'm doing, I don't say more than, "I'm going through a hard time right now. I'd appreciate your prayers."
4. If someone asks, "How can I pray for you?" I try to be specific without dishonoring my husband. ("Pray that he'll see God's hand on his life," not "Pray that he won't be such a creep.")

We were created with a need to talk, but God tells us that our speech must be without malice and slander; our words should build up, not tear down. My desire is to always be a woman of discretion. I want the people in whom I confide to be able to say, "She speaks well of her husband."

Lord,
As the proverb says,
"Like a gold ring in a pig's snout
Is a beautiful woman who shows no discretion"
    (Proverbs 11:22).
I confess that I haven't always been discreet
When it comes to confiding about my marriage.
It's a balancing act:
I feel the need to talk things out,
But I also don't want to embarrass my husband.
Sometimes I think I can't do both.
Help me, Lord, to muzzle my mouth when I should keep quiet.
Teach me to speak with discretion,
So that I can honor you, and my husband as well.
In Jesus' name.
Amen.

WHEN
WORDS HURT

―――――――― ❧ ――――――――

But thanks be to God! He
gives us the victory through
our Lord Jesus Christ.

1 CORINTHIANS 15:57

―――――――― ❧ ――――――――

"Y ou think you're so high and mighty, but you're nothing."
"You're sleeping with the pastor over at that church
you're going to, aren't you?"

"Get out of my face with that religious garbage."

"You make me sick."

Even in the best relationships spouses lose their tempers
and say unkind things they regret later. But when it becomes a
pattern, it's abuse. In his book *Loving Solutions*, Gary Chapman
says verbal abuse "destroys respect, trust, admiration and intimacy—all key ingredients of a healthy marriage." He adds that
verbal abuse is "warfare designed to punish the other person, to
place blame, or to justify one's own actions or decisions."

Not every non-Christian husband is verbally abusive, but
many times the tension in a spiritually unequal marriage acts as
a trigger, resulting in angry outbursts. When the Spirit of God
is working in a man's life convicting him of sin, he may lash out.
Darkness hates light (John 3:19–21).

Licensed counselor Brenda Waggoner often advises women
who are regularly faced with verbal assaults to calmly but firmly
put the "verbal hand grenades" back on their husbands. "Tell

him that if he decides to keep talking to you like that, then you will leave for awhile until he cools off."

She says if he doesn't have an audience, if he sees that his outbursts aren't working and the benefits he gets from his controlling behavior are removed, the hope is that he'll get the message and stop, or at least recognize that he needs help. Although we may be called to accept occasional verbal attacks as part of suffering for righteousness' sake, allowing a regular abuser to continue hurts him as well as the one being assaulted.

In either case, the victory is that God will give strength and power and sufficient grace to do the right and healthy thing. He doesn't promise that it will be easy, but he does promise he will be with us and that ultimately we will be victorious.

Lord,
Words hurt.
Abusive words crush my spirit,
Diminish my person,
Reduce me.
But you say you have plans to prosper me, not harm me
To give me hope and a future.
You are for me; I have worth.
So does my husband, Lord,
But he needs help—he needs your help.
Open his ears to hear his own words.
Don't let him blame anyone but himself!
Help him to see his abusive words are because of his sin.
Even so, let him know that there's hope for him—
Use even this to draw him to yourself.
Help me, too, not to be a victim,
But a victor.
Amen.

COURAGE IN A
FORTUNE COOKIE

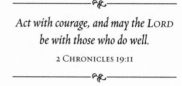

Act with courage, and may the LORD
be with those who do well.

2 CHRONICLES 19:11

I had only been a Christian a short time when confusion set in. I began doubting the truth of the gospel and the reality of my conversion. It seemed like every day I would get a visit from someone sharing their group's version of the truth. After they would leave, my mind would race with questions. *Is Christianity really the only way? Am I just being a religious nut? Is God even real?*

I knew my husband would've been much happier if I snapped out of whatever phase I was going through and returned to normal. As for me, I just wanted peace between us; more than anything, I hate conflict. I especially hate being the reason for it. So, I made a decision: I would go back to the way things were.

I had had a spiritual experience, but maybe it was just that, I reasoned. *Maybe it was like a dream and, like a dream, it was time for it to end. Time to wake up.*

I was in anguish. I didn't know what to do or what to believe. A friend from church assured me that doubting is normal, even healthy. She said the Lord would guide me into what's true. As I listened to her, something inside me urged me to stand firm. I didn't know then that it was God's Spirit encouraging me.

111

Still, as the sole Christian in my entire family at the time, to stand meant facing a possible future of conflict, and I was scared. I wrestled for days with what to do.

One night my husband and I went out for Chinese food. It had been a particularly stressful day between us, and I was looking for something, anything—a sign from God—to let me know what was true. What was *the* truth? That's when God sent his encouragement in a fortune cookie: "Have faith."

I don't believe in fortunes and magic, but I do believe that God comes to us at the exact moment we need him most with a word, a touch, a song, an inner strengthening of our spirit. He lets us know that he's really real and that following him is right. That he's the Truth, he's the only Way, and he's Life itself.

Have faith. O my soul, have faith.

Lord,
I need courage!
When I feel alone in my faith
And it seems easier to give up than to go on
And I'm confused and filled with doubt,
You come, bringing courage and encouragement with you.
I don't know how you do it;
I'm just thankful that you do.
You come just in time.
Always.
I love you, Lord,
For you care so very much for me.
Amen.

HE'S JEALOUS
OF GOD

*Jealousy arouses
a husband's fury.*

PROVERBS 6:34

Recently, a pastor-friend of mine and I were discussing what happens to a man when his wife loves Jesus and he doesn't understand. The only thing he knows is that one day she comes home all aglow and talking about Someone else, Someone he can't even see. She sings about him and wants to spend time with him. She tries to talk about him to her husband, but it sounds like gobbledy-gook to him.

And he's jealous. Sometimes quietly, other times openly angry.

My pastor-friend, who loves Jesus, said even as a Christian he sometimes feels pangs of jealousy when he thinks of his wife being the Bride of Christ. He thinks to himself, *She's my wife!* and knows he will have to confess his jealousy.

"It must be a thousand times worse for a man who's not a Christian," he said. "It would be easier if his wife was in love with another man. At least that he could understand and know how to compete."

As a pastor, he recommends that a woman in a spiritually unequal marriage not hide her love for the Lord but not to flaunt it either, as it tends to arouse a husband's jealousy.

On a positive note, he said a husband's feelings of jealousy shows that he cares enough about her that he's afraid of losing her. Then he added, "The best thing a woman can do for her husband is to assure and reassure him by her actions that loving Jesus means having an even greater love for him."

> *Jesus,*
> *You are the true Lover of my soul;*
> *You call me your bride*
> *And call yourself my Husband.*
> *How I love you!*
> *But my husband, the one here at home . . .*
> *He's so jealous of you,*
> *And I don't know what to do!*
> *I'm asking for your wisdom, Lord.*
> *I'm asking for a God-thing, a God-intervention,*
> *An entering into my husband's private feelings and insecurities*
> *To use them as you see fit,*
> *To teach him about you and himself.*
> *Help me also to be sensitive to his feelings*
> *That I may be the wife you want me to be.*
> *For your glory.*
> *Amen.*

BLESSED
FORGETFULNESS

*Forgive as the Lord
forgave you.*
COLOSSIANS 3:13

I have a terrible memory, which is both a burden and a blessing. It's a burden because I can never remember to buy trash bags or mail the electric bill. It's a blessing because I also tend to forget the arguments and squabbles my husband and I have experienced over the years.

The apostle Paul instructs us to "bear with each other and forgive whatever grievances you may have against each other. *Forgive as the Lord forgave you*" (Colossians 3:13, emphasis mine).

How has the Lord forgiven us? The prophet Jeremiah tells us that the Lord forgives our wickedness and remembers our sin no more (Jeremiah 31:34). He forgives and then he forgets.

As humans, we don't naturally forget, nor do we naturally forgive. But as Christians, we have the *super*natural ability to do so through the power of the Holy Spirit. It's been said that when someone reminded Red Cross founder Clara Barton of a past grievance done to her years before, she acted as if she had never heard of the incident. When someone pressed her, asking, "Don't you remember?" she replied, "No. I distinctly remember forgetting it."

In your relationship with your husband, what are some of the grievances that you're holding on to? Does he make fun of your faith? Has he promised to attend church or a Christian event, only to back out at the last minute?

Are you holding your spiritual inequality against him and blaming him for your feelings of discontent, dissatisfaction, and frustration?

Choose to forgive and then forget. If you do, what a tremendous witness that will be to an unbelieving husband.

Precious Jesus,
You forgave me,
Even as you hung upon the cross.
You chose to remember my sins no more.
How can I do less?
But I'm so human—
I don't forget easily the past and present hurts.
However, because you have given me your Spirit,
I can do all things.
I can forgive.
I can even forget.
Hallelujah, I can!
Amen.

STANDING
(NOT) ALONE

Therefore ... stand firm.
Let nothing move you.

1 CORINTHIANS 15:58

Standing for Christ isn't easy especially if your spouse isn't standing with you. When you feel alone in your faith, there's a real temptation to waver. To wimp out and compromise. *If I keep Jesus to myself, hide my Bible, not show any evidence of my faith, then maybe I'll be more comfortable. We'll have peace in our home. Get along better.*

Maybe if I go back to a few of my old ways, say a few swear words ... maybe if my husband sees me being just like everyone else, he'll think it's not so difficult to be a Christian and he'll be drawn to Christ quicker.

Ideas like that are tempting, but such compromises never work. In *No More Mr. Nice Guy,* Steve Brown describes a paradox in his life. He writes, "When I am too frightened to make waves for Christ, when I have chosen to go over in a corner and avoid conflict and problems, when I have chosen to take the easy way out, and when I have chosen to allow my faith to be insipid, I find that my anxiety level rises. In fact, that which I think will lessen my worry and anxiety does just the opposite. However, I have found that when I stand, God stands with me."

Standing for Christ doesn't mean being obnoxious, just true to who you are as an adopted child of God. Besides, when you stand for Christ, even in the midst of the conflict that it may bring, it demonstrates that he is, indeed, worthy.

Jesus told his disciples not to hide their lights under baskets but to shine them for him. The good news is, as we do, as we shine and stand firm, we don't stand alone. Jesus stands with us.

Lord,
As uncomfortable and lonely as it is sometimes
To stand for you—
Especially when my husband doesn't—
It's even more uncomfortable to compromise and waver.
How I need your help, Lord!
A battle rages inside of me:
I'm a coward; I'm weak.
I need your power and strength
To stand for you.
Help me to be true to who I am:
A called and chosen child
Who desperately needs her Father—
Her Father who tells her to stand and then stands with her ...
Forever!
Amen.

THE SILENT
TREATMENT

*In quietness and trust
is your strength.*

ISAIAH 30:15

I n *Chocolate Chili Pepper Love,* Becky Freeman writes about "Power Packed Quietness." She says silence can be a powerful response for a woman who is facing a husband whose anger is out of control and is beyond reasoning with.

However, the silence she describes is not a doormat silence but the silence of Christ as when he stood silently before Herod and Pontius Pilate. "This is a silence that conveys, 'I know I'm precious to God. My life is one of supreme respect: for God, for his creation, for you, and for myself,'" she writes.

When you have truth on your side, when you have *the* Truth (Jesus), you often don't need to speak at all. You don't need to defend yourself; truth is its own defense. Truth allows you to remain calm in the heat of conflict and quiet in the face of opposition.

The Bible teaches that there is a time and a season for everything, including a time to speak and a time to be silent (Ecclesiastes 3:7). Even so, whatever the season, as Christians, our method of communication needs to be one of respect and not manipulation. That means no:

- Martyred sighs as you get yourself and the kids dressed for church as your husband stays in bed.
- Dirty looks at your husband because of his beer-drinking, swearing, smoking, and so on.
- Cold shoulders that say, "You want me to keep quiet about my faith? I'll show you quiet."
- Keeping your distance so your husband's unbelief won't "rub off" on you.

Whether it is with silence or with spoken words, our communication needs to convey the message: "I love you, God loves us both, and we are both worthy of respect."

Lord,
You say there is a time to speak and a time to be silent,
But too often my "silent treatment" yells out a message
Of contempt
Of judgment
Of manipulation and revenge.
But you want my silence to be a message
Of power
Of strength
Of love and calm assurance
And quiet trust.
Once again, I come to you in desperate need.
(How grateful I am that you never turn me away!)
I can't do this unless you do it first in me,
And then through me.
Lord, may my words, both spoken and unspoken,
Be pleasing to you.
Amen.

WAITING WITH
A PATIENT HEART

❧

Being strengthened with all
power according to his glorious
might so that you may have
great endurance and patience . . .

COLOSSIANS 1:11

❧

When it comes to waiting, how long is "long enough"? When it comes to waiting patiently, how patient does God expect a woman to be as she prays for the spiritual growth of her husband?

One woman who has been praying for more than twenty-five years for her husband to come to faith in Christ said, "People keep telling me to be patient. Well, you know what? I'm so patient I could scream!"

Jeanne Zornes, author of *When I Prayed for Patience . . . God Let Me Have It!*, says, "The hardest part of waiting is 'just before.' Just before you see the answer. Just before you're ready to give up. Just before it all breaks open, and you understand."

She adds, "Fussing doesn't get you what you want. Fussing only reveals that we cannot accept the circumstances God has put us in. It is a symptom of an inner state of [the] soul that has not come to rest with God."

Patience isn't a gritting of the teeth to keep from screaming out of frustration, but a calmness and an unwavering confidence that God knows what he's doing and has a good reason for not granting us what we ask when we ask for it. That includes as noble a request as asking for a husband's salvation.

During times of frustration and impatience, it helps to know that:

- He who began a good work in us (and in our families) will finish what he has started (Philippians 1:6).
- God is not slow in keeping his promises (2 Peter 3:9).
- He has made everything beautiful in his time (Ecclesiastes 3:11).
- He is able to make all grace abound to us (2 Corinthians 9:8), which includes developing perseverance when we want to quit and an inner calm when we're so patient that we want to scream.

Father,
Waiting is so difficult
And my patience grows so thin.
Perseverance sounds like a dirty word.
Perseverance isn't fun.
I don't want to persevere!
Yet I know that it's through waiting and trusting that my
     character grows.
Trusting in you.
Trusting that, while I wait, you are at work:
In me
In my husband
In our family.
As for how long I must wait,
I know the answer:
As long as it takes, and no longer.
Amen.

LOVING WITH FORBEARANCE

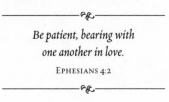

*Be patient, bearing with
one another in love.*

EPHESIANS 4:2

A friend called the other day. She's a fairly new Christian, married to a man who's not too sure what to think about her faith. They're both uneasy around each other.

I asked her how she was doing. "Great!" she said. "I have so much patience with him."

Then she laughed. "Of course, he's out of town this week. Ask me next week and I'm sure I'll have a different answer."

It's one thing to be patient with a situation, but quite another to be patient with a person, especially one with whom you differ fundamentally. However, as Christians we're called to bear with one another, and as wives, God calls us to bear with our husbands. Patiently bearing with one another "in love."

Another word the Bible uses for patience is "forbearance." It goes beyond merely tolerating a person or "hanging tough" in a situation such as an unequally yoked marriage. It has the idea of a patience that is merciful, charitable, and grace-filled. It's harmonious and humble. It genuinely loves and honors another, despite differences.

How is that possible? Not by willpower or sheer grit. Rather, it's a fruit, or a by-product, of the Spirit of God in a believer's life. As we yield to the Spirit, who always forbears with us, he develops that same quality in us.

What does forbearance look like? You'll recognize it when:

- Your husband's pointed barbs about your faith tempt you to respond in anger but you don't. Instead, you stand firm and offer the grace of Jesus because your husband "knows not what he is doing" (see Luke 23:34).
- Just when his seeming indifference drives you to the point of despair, you opt instead to rest in knowing that God is not finished yet.
- As his unredeemed behavior and thinking causes you to fear his future, you trade your fear and worry for the enveloping, perfect love of God that casts out all fear.

We can bear with one another in love . . . because God bears with us.

Father,
When my love grows thin,
Yours is abundant—
For me, in me, and through me.
And because your love is forbearing,
I can likewise forbear.
I can go on . . . patiently.
You never said it would be easy,
But you did say it would be possible.
Thank you for your precious promises;
Thank you for your powerful Word.
Thank you for your enabling Holy Spirit.
Thank you for your patient love.
Amen.

I'M ANGRY, LORD!

An angry [woman] stirs up
dissension, and a hot-tempered
one commits many sins.

PROVERBS 29:22

Sometimes it seethes below the surface and shows itself in clenched teeth and narrowed eyes, or a closet door closing a bit too hard as you get yourself ready for church while *he* remains a lump under the covers.

Sometimes it shows itself in harsh, judgmental words. He calls you a "Jesus freak," and you retaliate by calling him a "godless heathen" or words to that effect.

You lash out at his behavior, even his character. You can't help it, or so you think. You think your husband's rejection of spiritual things is done out of spite, that he's doing it just to tick you off. You may even put up a wall that says, "If you reject the gospel, then I reject you."

You think your anger is "righteous anger." It is, but it's *self-*righteous, and self-righteous anything is always sin and stems from a desire to be in control and to have things go your own way.

There's a time and a place and good reasons for anger in a marriage, but not getting your own way isn't one of them. It's frustrating to stand by as your husband rejects the gospel, the very answer to his needs. It's frustrating to wait and wait and wait. Frustration easily turns to anger, and anger quickly turns to sin.

But God is able.

He is able to refresh us when we're weary and renew us when we're weak.

He is able to quiet our frustrations and turn them into faith.

He is even able to take our anger and do something miraculous.

He's able to turn it into love.

Lord,
Sometimes I'm just so angry!
And even though I know it's wrong,
I direct it toward my husband.
I want him to be a Christian!
I want my life to be different! I want it now!
(Don't I sound like a spoiled child?)
I'm grateful that you don't condemn me for my angry feelings.
Instead,
You invite me to bring them to you,
To confess them as the sin that they are,
And to walk away
Calmed, comforted, and forgiven.
Thank you for your Spirit who convicts me
And your grace that frees me.
Thank you, Lord, for your love that quiets even my
angriest heart.
Amen.

THANKS IN
ALL THINGS

---ॐ---

Give thanks in all circumstances,
for this is God's will for you
in Christ Jesus.

1 THESSALONIANS 5:18

---ॐ---

How thankful are you in your circumstances? *Well, I guess things could be worse. But I'd be more thankful if my husband would (go to church, pray with me, read the Bible, not make fun of my faith).*

Sound familiar? But God's will for us as Christians is to give thanks in all circumstances. No qualifiers, limits, or conditions. We are to give thanks in all circumstances, even the hard ones.

Jonah knew about hard circumstances. When the ancient prophet found himself inside the belly of a fish, with no escape hatch handy and seaweed wrapped around his head, the Bible says he praised God for bringing his life "up from the pit" (Jonah 2:6) and offered him "a song of thanksgiving" (v. 9).

If anyone had reason to qualify his thanksgiving, it was Jonah. As far as circumstances go, things probably couldn't get much worse than his. Yet even in his underwater prison, he gave thanks.

When your marriage isn't the one you long for, it's easy to find reasons to not be thankful. Your husband may be cold, indifferent, hostile to your faith, rude to your friends. He may make your life a living hell as you try to live your faith and he tries to trip you up. How, then, can you possibly give thanks in these circumstances?

A friend of mine once decided to take the "thanksgiving challenge." She determined to list a hundred reasons to give thanks in her spiritually unequal marriage. She said the first twenty were the most difficult because she was still focusing on her circumstances. But once she started focusing on God and his goodness to her, she had a hard time ending her list at a hundred.

Not all circumstances are good, but God is good in all our circumstances. So take the "thanksgiving challenge" and see how long your list can be.

Father,
When all I can see are my circumstances,
The challenges and difficulties,
The heartaches and hard times,
I find it difficult to give thanks.
Then I remember your goodness to me,
Your lovingkindness and your care.
That's when my heart overflows with thanksgiving.
That's when my thanks turns from a sacrificial offering
To words of exuberant worship.
Oh, thank you, Lord!
In all things, I thank you, Lord.
Amen.

Psalm of
Thanksgiving

Give thanks to the LORD,
for he is good;
his love endures forever.

PSALM 106:1

One way to cultivate a thankful heart is by creating your own psalm, such as this one:

Thank you, Lord, for this marriage you have placed me in and for opportunities to stretch and grow. Thank you for the privilege of being your ambassador to someone who doesn't yet know you and for the peace that you bring to my soul.

Thank you for whisker hairs in the bathroom sink because they belong to the face of someone you love. Thank you for sincere, even challenging, arguments about faith because they serve to draw me into your Word for answers.

Thank you for kisses in the kitchen and touch football in the yard. Thank you for friends who pray and do not pry and for glimpses of your Spirit at work. Thank you, Lord, for your surprises of grace, for answers to prayer, for unexpected blessings, for longings fulfilled.

Thank you for your faithfulness in my waiting, your presence in my loneliness.

When my situation grows hard, you continue to be good. In my darkness, you remain my light. You are my hope, my strength, my rock. You dry my tears and give me reason to smile.

Thank you, Lord, for all the times I think I can't go on, yet I do. Thank you for pushing me and prodding me, stretching my faith and strengthening my endurance.

Because I've cried, I've known your comfort. Because I've struggled, I've known your tender care. You have given me this husband to love and have kept me in this unequal yoke as a calling, as a ministry, even as a gift.

You see me. You know me. You hear my prayers and fill my heart with hope. You know what you are doing, and you do all things well. I can trust you; I can rest.

Oh, thank you, Lord, I can rest. I give you praise, my Savior and my God.

> *Heavenly Father,*
> *There is so much in my life to be thankful for!*
> *(Remind me next time I'm tempted to forget.)*
> *Most of all, I give thanks to you*
> *For choosing me*
> *For calling me*
> *For saving me.*
> *Thank you, Lord,*
> *Amen!*

GOD LOVES THE WORD *IMPOSSIBLE*

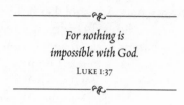

*For nothing is
impossible with God.*

LUKE 1:37

A few weeks before Easter Sunday my pastor asked us to write down the names of five people we wanted to see come to church on Easter and then pray for them every day. Then, as if he read my mind, he said, "If you think there's someone impossible for God to reach, then you don't know God; you don't know what he's able and willing to do in a person's life."

I just shook my head as I wrote down my five names. I even laughed as I wrote several of them. *I know God,* I thought, *but . . .*

That got me thinking about possibilities. I have no trouble believing that God made the universe out of nothing and that Jesus changed water into wine. I believe in the resurrection and the virgin birth; I even believe a fish swallowed the prophet Jonah.

But I'm still not too sure about some of the names I'd written down.

Once Jesus walked into a home where a little girl had just died. He told the mourners, "She's not dead; she's just asleep."

But they knew better. They knew an impossible situation when they saw one. They knew dead. However, they didn't know God. They didn't know the One standing in front of them

131

was God himself, who simply walked over to the dead girl and raised her back to life, as if there was nothing to it.

That's the point, isn't it?

Who knows, maybe a long time ago someone wrote down my name and shook her head. Maybe she laughed to think that God could ever change me. Maybe her pastor said, "If you think she's impossible, then you don't know God."

As Jesus told his doubting disciples, "With God all things are possible" (Matthew 19:26).

All things. Even the salvation of the one I love.

Lord,
It's as if you love to do the impossible,
Defy logic, go beyond even the extraordinary.
You are a God of miracles;
You transform human hearts.
No one is beyond your reach.
No one is too hard for you to change.
No one is impossible for you to redeem.
So once again I pray for the one I love
And leave him in your sovereign care.
You are Lord of the impossible.
Help me to believe—
I do believe!
Amen.

LOVING A NEGATIVE SPOUSE

Love ... always hopes,
always perseveres.

1 CORINTHIANS 13:7

In the tales of Winnie the Pooh, a sad-sack donkey named Eeyore never sees blue skies or green grass, only doom and gloom. His philosophy of life is, "Why bother? Nothing good will happen anyway."

Such philosophy might be cute coming from a fictional character, but what if that character lives in your house? What if it's your husband whose chin is always dragging in the dirt? A negative spouse can be critical and controlling, a victim, a pessimist. He might demand perfection from everyone around him, be withdrawn and sulking, or just plain sad.

Even Christians can be negative, but they have the Holy Spirit within and the resources of prayer and the Word of God to combat their negativity and transform their thought processes. An unbelieving husband doesn't have these resources; however, as his believing wife, you do.

Marriage and family counselor Tim Gardner writes about loving a negative spouse in an issue of *Marriage Partnership*. With one couple he counseled, he instructed the nonnegative spouse to refrain from arguing or name-calling. Instead, the spouse was to point out lovingly how many of the other person's negative predictions of the past had not come true and to carefully encourage giving new ideas a chance. Above all, the nonnegative spouse was to offer constant reassurance of her love and commitment, demonstrating daily the promise of Christ never to leave or forsake those he loves.

In the Hundred Acre Woods, Eeyore's friends never abandon him. Even so, the donkey remains negative, which is always a possibility with a negative spouse. As Gardner points out, change is never guaranteed. However, for those who do what they can to make their marriages better and commit to loving their negative mates for the long haul without expectation of a return, they do receive a positive return. "Even if that return was only a peace within themselves that comes from loving a mate as God intended," he writes.

Living with a negative spouse is emotionally draining; misery tends to love company, and negative people tend to bring others down with them. But because God loves us in our own negativity, we can do the same, because we do it with God's love and not our own.

Father,
Open my eyes to my own negativity
And all the ways I've contributed to that of my husband.
Show me ways to love him, to offer him hope—
The hope that is in you.
Use this situation to draw me closer to you and closer to him,
Even if he pushes me away.
Open his eyes, too, Lord, that he might see the possibilities
*   and blessings*
That a life in Christ brings.
Bring him to a place
Where he is willing to exchange his negativity for everything
*   you have for him:*
Eternal peace, eternal hope, eternal life.
Amen.

ETHICAL SHADES OF GRAY

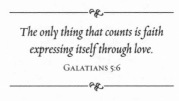

*The only thing that counts is faith
expressing itself through love.*

GALATIANS 5:6

When it comes to "big" sins like armed robbery, getting drunk, and murder, the Bible is explicit: Thou shalt not. We know what to do when confronted with blatant sin—say no and run.

Not too many husbands present their wives with "big sin" propositions. But what about those questionable situations that aren't black and white or are "tiny" sins? Your husband likes to tell off-color jokes; he uses bad language, eats candy from the bins at the market without paying for it, or takes pens from work. As a Christian wife, what should you do?

Gary Oliver, executive director of the Center for Marriage and Family Studies at John Brown University, offers the following advice.

Avoid knee-jerk reactions. Think and pray things through and consider past confrontations: What worked (or didn't work) then? Don't confront at the moment, especially in public, and never attack.

Communicate as an individual. Say, "This is the conviction I have." That allows you to state your beliefs without forcing your faith or being "weird for Jesus." You can't expect a non-Christian to behave as a Christian.

Don't make a big deal of it. Especially with off-color jokes or conversation topics, Oliver suggests offering a simple, "I'd prefer not to hear it." He adds, "Tell a joke of your own. For men, humor is a way of showing affection."

Be flexible. Tolerate things that may be distasteful as long as it doesn't cause you to sin.

Appeal to your spouse's sense of fair play. When it comes to issues involving the children, approach your mate on the basis of what's fair. ("I know you don't want your son stealing, and he looks to you as a role model.") Most unbelieving spouses are eventually fair when it comes to their kids.

Pray, pray, pray.

Father,
You have me in this marriage
To be a light in the darkness.
But sometimes the darkness is merely gray—
No definite contrast,
No lines,
No "Thou shalts" or "Thou shalt nots."
Give me wisdom, Lord, in these gray-shaded areas.
Help me to do the loving thing,
The right thing,
In faith,
Trusting you to guide and direct me.
Help me to communicate my convictions
Without being "holier than thou."
You never said this would be easy,
Only that I can do all things through Christ,
And that you would be faithful
To see me through.
Amen.

SUNDAY MORNING STRUGGLE

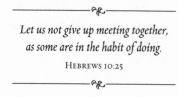

Let us not give up meeting together,
as some are in the habit of doing.

HEBREWS 10:25

When a person comes to faith in Christ, one of the first-fruits is a desire to meet with other believers. We are a family, created for corporate worship with our Christian brothers and sisters. However, when you're alone in your faith and your husband doesn't attend church with you, Sunday mornings are often a battlefield. Even with a husband who is supportive of your faith (as long as you leave him out of it), the battlefield is internal. *I love my church; I love my husband. Should I go or should I stay home?*

Sometimes a wife encounters open hostility. She may go to church, but she "pays" for it when she gets home with a cold shoulder or snide remarks. The temptation is to give up, give in, compromise. *Maybe I can be a Christian without going to church.*

Although going to church doesn't make a person a Christian, regular church attendance nourishes a believer. The writer of Hebrews calls believers to persevere and to hold on to the hope we profess. When we meet together, we remind each other of God's faithfulness and then "spur one another on toward love and good deeds."

We can't do the Christian life alone. Unless we meet regularly with like-minded believers, we won't persevere; we'll lose hope and forget about God's faithfulness. We'll fall away and forget about grace.

One woman said, "It's not always easy when my husband gives me a hard time, but when I think about all the Christians around the world who are persecuted and even killed for their faith, snide remarks from my husband are nothing in comparison."

No matter what the circumstances, when we meet together for worship, we gain encouragement and courage. We may be called to "pay" for it when we get home, but even then God goes with us. He won't forsake us.

With God's grace, we can persevere; we can endure. We can even pay any price asked because Christ already paid it all for us.

Father,
You see my situation; you know my struggles.
You hear the arguments and feel the tension.
Lord, my heart is torn!
A battle rages inside me and no matter what I decide,
A part of me suffers.
Help me not to give up meeting for worship.
Oh, how I need my brothers and sisters at church!
Help me find creative solutions
To these Sunday morning struggles
Without compromising my relationship with you.
It isn't easy, Lord.
But neither is it impossible.
(And in my struggle, I haven't had to shed blood.)
I offer these Sunday battles to you, Lord,
As a willing sacrifice.
For you are God! And I am yours.
Amen.

SETTING AN EXAMPLE
FOR MY KIDS

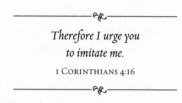

*Therefore I urge you
to imitate me.*

1 CORINTHIANS 4:16

A s my two daughters grew up, I often wondered what they
thought about marriage. From being raised in church, they
knew that God's ideal is one man, one woman, and their children all in agreement in matters of faith. But in our family, their
dad didn't share our faith.

As the mom, my feelings and thoughts ran the gamut. I worried that somehow I was setting a bad example because our family wasn't God's ideal. I felt guilty because I wasn't providing my
children with God's best. I feared that they would marry unbelievers themselves, since that's what they were used to in our
family. Even though my husband and I were both unbelievers
when we got married, I still felt guilty.

Eventually I came to accept that I could only do my best to
be an example of a Christian wife and trust that God would fill
in the gap. Still, sometimes I wondered about what kind of an
example I was setting for my girls.

Just before my older daughter got married (to a Christian
man!), I asked her what she had learned about marriage from
watching her dad and me. After some thought she said, "I've
learned that it's not always easy and that when things get

139

tough, not to give up or give in because tough times don't last forever."

She said she also learned that love doesn't leave when things aren't perfect.

As a mom, I can only do what I can do. I will always be imperfect and I will always fall far short of what I can and should be. Not only that, circumstances will never be ideal. Even in families where everyone is a Christian, life isn't ideal.

What I want my daughters to see from my example as a wife is someone who trusts God with her circumstances and leans hard on him for grace. That includes trusting God with my example to my children. Because he's committed to me and committed to them, regardless of the circumstances, it is possible to impact my children positively for God's kingdom.

Father,
From before eternity began,
You knew how my family would be.
You knew the example I would be to my children
And how much I would need you to work in and through me.
You, Lord, have been faithful
Even when I have not.
When I've doubted, you have encouraged me.
When I've worried, you have calmed my fears.
Through your Holy Spirit,
You have enabled my children to see through my failings to
*   your faithfulness.*
May they always see in me
An example of simple trust in a God who can do the impossible.
Amen.

He Ain't Heavy,
He's My Husband

---❦---

*Carry each other's burdens,
and in this way you will fulfill
the law of Christ.*

GALATIANS 6:2

---❦---

Two times in my marriage I faced a bleak future. During both times my husband seemed to wrestle with hopelessness and despair. He retreated into himself and lost his sparkle. He hated coming home and often talked about leaving.

Each time he would assure me his wanting to leave had nothing to do with me or our girls; he was just tired. He talked about regrets and longings. He talked about guilt and how he wanted so much more for me than he thought he was able to give. "No matter what happens, I'll always love you," he would say. I knew he meant it, although it didn't comfort me.

He worried that he was a burden to me. He wanted me to find another husband, a Christian husband. "You deserve it," he'd say.

Those were dark days. I can only describe them as if the gates of hell opened up and dumped on us.

During those times I clung to the promise that, as God's beloved, I was and am "more than [a conqueror] through him who loved us" (Romans 8:37) and that God was "able to do immeasurably more" than I could ever ask or imagine (Ephesians 3:20). He sustained me through those times as only he can do; he carried me as I helped carry my husband.

As I look back, each time of darkness ended almost instantaneously. One day my husband was in despair, the next he found the hope he needed to go on.

"Why did you put up with me?" he asked me after the last time.

"Because I love you," I answered. However, it goes much deeper than that. I realize now that I "put up" with him, not just because I love him, but because God loves him and long ago chose me to be a channel of his grace to this man. His love compels me to bear all things, believe all things, hope all things, and endure all things.

No matter how God asks me to minister to my husband, it's never too burdensome. He ain't heavy at all—he's my husband.

Lord,
When my husband hurts, I hurt.
I know I shouldn't worry—
You always have us both securely in your hands—
But sometimes I do.
Sometimes I feel powerless to help him, powerless to help
    myself as well.
It's scary, Lord.
The darkness is so scary.
But you are my light and my salvation,
And you will see me through even the darkest times.
Protect my husband, Lord.
May the burdens he carries bring him to his knees,
That he may once and for all
Lay them at the foot of your cross.
In Jesus' name I pray.
Amen.

LEAN ON ME

A friend loves at all times,
and a brother is born for adversity.

PROVERBS 17:17

I don't remember exactly how Terry and I met, but she was my lifeline during the first few years after I became a Christian. We attended the same church in Portland, Maine, both of us without our husbands.

C. S. Lewis once described the birth of friendship as the moment one person says to another, "What! You too? I thought I was the only one." Meeting Terry was like that. When I was with her, I was no longer alone in my faith.

We understood each other's tears of impatience and frustration. We prayed together and studied the Bible together. We laughed and cried together. When she said, "I understand how you feel," I knew she did—and I understood how she felt as well.

God never meant for us to go through life alone, although alone is how you may often feel, especially when you're the only Christian in your marriage. We all need mentors and examples, and we need comrades, fellow-strugglers. Picture a three-legged race, with two friends bound together, helping each other move forward. That's what Terry was for me for the two years I lived in Maine.

Do you have a Terry in your life? Look around your church and ask God to direct you to someone with whom you can say, "You too? I thought I was the only one!" Once you find her and before you begin a friendship, keep these guidelines in mind:

- Vow never to trade "my husband's a jerk" stories. Share feelings while protecting your husband's character.
- Guard yourself from making your friendship the priority relationship in your life. Your husband and family come before friends.
- Pray with and for each other. Pray for each other's husband, especially when you feel discouraged. It's often easier to pray for someone else.
- Keep your friendship Christ-centered. Advice to each other needs to be biblical.

Lord,
You have created us to need one another.
To rejoice with those who rejoice
And mourn with those who mourn.
To carry each other's burdens,
Walk together,
Spur each other on toward love and good deeds.
Help me to find a friend
And to be a friend,
To be an encouragement even as I am encouraged.
Thank you, Lord,
That you never meant for us to walk to heaven alone.
Amen.

INCLUDING DAD

All this is from God, who reconciled
us to himself through Christ and
gave us the ministry of reconciliation.

2 CORINTHIANS 5:18

When it comes to your family dynamics, is your husband "odd man out"? When faith divides a family, it's easy to play three, four, five against one. Not that it's done intentionally, but when you and your children's lives center around Christ and the church and your husband's life doesn't, he's left behind.

In our family, with two daughters and no sons, my husband says he sometimes feels like an alien around all the "girlie stuff." He still can't figure out eyelash curlers. Christianity only makes things even more alienating at times.

As Christians we've been given the ministry of reconciliation, reconciling people first to God but also to each other, starting with those living in our own homes. So, where do you start?

If there's a wall of separation that seems impenetrable in your house, start small. Start with things you and your children have in common with your husband. Does he enjoy playing catch in the yard? Ice cream cones at the mall? Is there a project the whole family can do together?

Include your husband in as many activities and conversations as you can. Be prepared to have him balk at or rebuff your efforts, especially if your alienation has included hard feelings.

By reaching out to include your husband in your family activities, you will show him that God's love is inclusive and has the power to cover a multitude of sins and to bring the faraway close.

Father,
You know the struggles I go through
Trying to keep my family together.
I feel pulled trying to be wife, mother, Christian.
I want peace;
I want us to be a family
But sometimes it feels as if I'm trying to reach across the
      Grand Canyon
Or trying to find common ground with an alien from
      another planet.
Lord, help me to be a bridge in my family;
Empower me with your love
To be the minister of reconciliation you've called me to be.
For my husband's sake, my children's sake,
For the sake of our family,
For your name's sake.
Amen.

"BUT DAD DOESN'T
HAVE TO GO . . ."

---❧---

*I have been reminded of your
sincere faith, which first lived in
your grandmother Lois and in your
mother Eunice and, I am persuaded,
now lives in you also.*

2 TIMOTHY 1:5

---❧---

Whether your unbelieving husband is supportive or antagonistic of your bringing the children to church and raising them in the Christian faith, there may come a Sunday morning when one or more of your children decides to follow their dad's example. *"But Dad doesn't have to go to church."*

As if being in a spiritually mismatched marriage isn't difficult enough, a child who wants to find life apart from Christ only adds to a woman's struggles. *Am I not a good role model? If I insist my child attend church and youth group, will I drive him further away from the faith? If I don't insist, will I be sending the message that faith isn't important?*

A Christian mother "must ensure that she neither compromises her convictions nor alienates her children from herself by forcing them to go to church," writes minister and author Michael Fanstone in *Raising Kids Christian When Your Husband Doesn't Believe.*

He says a woman is responsible before God for encouraging her children to attend church for as long as she can. "Such encouragement, as long as it is not heavy-handed and dictatorial, can make a dramatic impact on youngsters, even if they abandon going to church earlier in life than their Christian mother would choose."

If it's any consolation, children who grow up with two committed Christian parents often walk away from the faith for a season too. But God is faithful. He listens to the prayers of a mother's heart. In his time, he answers them too.

Lord,
My heart's greatest desire
Is to have my children walking with you
In their own vital faith.
Likewise,
My greatest fear is that they won't.
How easily I forget
That you keep your hand on my life,
On my children's lives.
I forget that you are a God
Who watches over and guides those whom you have redeemed.
I forget that neither I nor my children can go anywhere
Out of your knowledge and providential care.
I entrust my children to you, Lord,
For you care for them even more than I do.
To you, I commit their spiritual future.
To you, I commit my own.
Amen.

A Word
Aptly Spoken

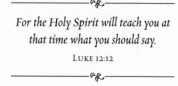

*For the Holy Spirit will teach you at
that time what you should say.*

LUKE 12:12

For the most part, women living with unbelieving husbands
are to refrain from talking about their faith. To a man, unso-
licited advice and "preaching" from his wife conveys the message, "I think you're incompetent." He tunes out the words and
puts up his defenses, or he goes on the offensive. God knew this
when he inspired the apostle Peter to instruct wives to win their
non-Christian husbands "without a word." Sometimes, however,
God opens doors and windows of opportunity for a wife to
speak.

A friend's father-in-law died and left her husband an inher-
itance, which came at a time they were deeply in debt and her
husband couldn't see any hope in their situation. One night,
overcome with grief and gratitude concerning his dad, he said
to her, "Someone had to die to give me life."

My friend said she gasped. Her heart pounded as she
debated whether or not to say anything. Sensing this was an
open door to speak, she said, "That's the gospel!"

Her husband had gone to church with her before and had
heard the gospel preached, so she knew she didn't have to say
anything more. She knew that in conversations with men, often

less is more. Although my friend's husband didn't reply, that doesn't mean God won't use her words toward her husband's spiritual transformation.

St. Francis of Assisi said, "Preach the gospel at all times. If necessary, use words." Mostly we preach with our lives, but every once in awhile God gives us words to speak. How precious a gift that is.

Father,
You created women with a desire to talk—
And then instructed us not to!
How ironic.
But Lord, you know best.
You know how to reach my husband better than I do.
You know whose words he will receive and whose he will reject.
You also know that one of my greatest joys
Is sharing your gospel truth
With the one I love most on earth.
Please give me the wisdom to know when to speak and when
    to keep silent.
I pray that every word I speak in witness to you
Will bear much fruit in my husband's life,
That my words may be as the proverb says,
"Like apples of gold in settings of silver."
May every word I speak be only for your glory.
Amen.

GOD IS ABLE

———— ❧ ————

"Do you believe that I am
able to do this?"
"Yes, Lord," they replied.

MATTHEW 9:28

———— ❧ ————

When Jesus was on earth, he healed the blind, the lame, and the sick. He raised the dead. Two thousand years later he is still able to do all that and more. He is able to intervene, restore, and redeem any situation. He is able to sustain you and cause you to thrive even in your unequally yoked marriage.

God is able to keep you, guide you, comfort you, and encourage you. He is able to help you raise your children in the faith and direct your unbelieving husband as you submit to him. He "is able to make all grace abound to you" (2 Corinthians 9:8) and give you sufficient grace for every sorrow, every lonely Sunday morning, every disagreement about faith, every heartache because the one you love doesn't understand.

When your prayers seem to go unanswered, God is able to draw you close and give you hope. When things look bleak, God is able to do the unimaginable, to do immeasurably more than what we ask or think possible (Ephesians 3:20).

Just ask Cindy.

Emotionally and physically exhausted from trying to raise her two young children in the faith while dealing with an unbelieving husband who was also a drug addict, Cindy had reached a breaking point. One afternoon, with her husband gone and the kids down for a nap, she went outside to mow the lawn. When the mower wouldn't start, she broke down sobbing. Looking skyward she yelled, "Where are you, God? I don't know how much more I can take!"

Not ten seconds later, an older man on a tractor lawnmower drove around the bend on her street and stopped to help her. She didn't recognize him right away, but later she knew God had come to her rescue. He had heard her cries and came to her disguised as a man on a riding lawnmower. Cindy says, "That one incident convinced me that God is able to take care of me, no matter what happens with my marriage."

God is able to fight our battles and right the wrongs we suffer. He is able to bring light into our darkness and hope in our despair. But not only is he able to do all that and more, he is willing. Oh, how we need to remember that!

Lord,
You are, indeed, able to do anything.
When I am worried and afraid, you give me courage and hope.
You provide for my needs, bolster my spirit.
Whenever I start to doubt your goodness
And your ability to work in my husband's heart—
To work in my heart—
You always prove me wrong and prove yourself able.
Because you are able, I can persevere.
I can do whatever it is that you call me to do,
I can love my husband sacrificially,
Wait patiently for his salvation,
I can trust; I can relax, because you, Lord, are able.
Amen.

BETWEEN
TWO LOVES

When my husband and I first got married, we were perfectly, equally yoked: We were both unbelievers. We had
our struggles, but not about matters of faith since neither of us
thought much about it.

Then God intervened in our lives.

At the time I was not actively seeking the Lord, but he was
passionately pursuing me. My conversion came as if out of
nowhere. One minute I didn't care two bits about God, and the
next I was madly, deeply in love with him. The problem was,
my husband didn't share my same passion.

I felt torn—torn between two loves. In many ways I felt like
I was carrying on an illicit love affair. I loved my husband ...
but I loved Jesus, too. I could share my love for my husband
with Jesus, but I couldn't share my love for Jesus with my husband—he wasn't interested. So as best I could, I tried to keep
my loves separate, although it only made me miserable.

I felt guilty sneaking off to spend time with Jesus, the lover
of my soul. I didn't know how to love him with all my heart and
soul, my strength and mind, and also to love my husband. Back

then, I mistakenly thought it was an "either/or" proposition: I could *either* love Jesus *or* I could love my husband—but not both at the same time.

However, I was wrong. It's not "either/or"; it's "because." *Because* I love Jesus, or more accurately, because Jesus loves me, his love enables me to love others, even—and especially—my husband.

Jesus said that the greatest commandment is to love God completely and the second is to love others. He didn't say it would be easy, but he did say we could do both.

Gracious Lord,
You alone know my heart.
You know how I wrestle between loving you and loving
*   my husband.*
He feels it, too, Lord.
He senses that my heart is divided,
And that must hurt him.
The psalmist prayed for an undivided heart,
One that loves you completely,
One that is completely loved by you.
Me, too!
I want a heart that's not torn between two loves.
I want a heart that's whole and able to love you as well as
*   love others,*
Especially my husband, my precious "other."
Lord, you have called me to love him,
And I will—I can.
Because.
Because you love me
I can love both you and him.
Amen.

CALLED TO
MINISTRY

---

*For we are God's workmanship,
created in Christ Jesus to
do good works, which God prepared
in advance for us to do.*

EPHESIANS 2:10

When a person comes to faith in Christ, God gives supernatural gifts with which to serve him and others. He also gives us a desire to use these gifts in service to him. However, for those with unbelieving husbands who may not understand or support this desire, it's easy to become discouraged and resentful. *I could serve God if it wasn't for him.*

Although a woman's primary ministry is in the home with her own husband and children, often there's a desire to reach beyond the borders of the home with the gifts God has given. After all, he created us in Christ to do good works and has even prepared them in advance for us to do.

My friend Terry's unbelieving husband tolerated her going to church on Sunday mornings, but that was all. He didn't want her working in the nursery or teaching Sunday school or singing in the choir. He controlled the family finances, so she couldn't use any of the household money for ministry.

She didn't drive; she didn't work. She stayed home, caring for her husband and their two small children. Although her marital situation was constricting, Terry chose to view it as an adventure and didn't let it hinder her from finding a ministry outside her home.

As she prayed about what she could do, she realized that the one area in which she had complete freedom was her kitchen. She would stock her shelves with ingredients for cakes, cookies, and muffins, and while her husband was at work, she would bake all morning. In the afternoon, with her kids in their stroller, she would deliver her baked goods to her neighbors and share the gospel with them. Plus, when her husband came home, fresh-baked goodies awaited him.

Likewise, God has a ministry for each one of us. Some teach Sunday school, some go on mission trips, and some are called to serve with a batch of snickerdoodles. Go ahead and ask God for your ministry. After all, he's already prepared it in advance, just for you.

Lord,
You say if I delight myself in you,
You will give me the desires of my heart.
Because you are my delight,
Because your love has so captured me,
The desire of my heart is to tell others about you.
I know you have called me to minister to my family first;
I also know that in my sphere of influence,
In my world,
You have created good works for me to perform,
And that no ministry in your service is too small.
Whatever you have for me to do,
May I do it for your glory.
In Jesus' name.
Amen.

WHAT SPECIES
IS YOUR MATE?

---

*When they heard about the
resurrection of the dead, some of them
sneered, but others said, "We want to
hear you again on this subject."*

ACTS 17:32

In *Surviving a Spiritual Mismatch in Marriage,* authors Lee and Leslie Strobel write about discerning a mate's receptivity to the gospel before attempting to share one's faith. They list four "species" of nonbelievers: *cynics, skeptics, spectators,* and *seekers.*

Cynics are often antagonistic and unapproachable. For spiritually cynical husbands, the Strobels suggest asking questions such as, "What happened to make you so angry about the topic of God?" Then listen with empathy and without judgment. By listening and not preaching, you become "safe."

Skeptics may be interested in spiritual matters, but their doubts get in the way. The Strobels suggest encouraging a skeptic to list his doubts into specific questions. "With your spouse's list as a starting point, you can now pinpoint the roadblocks between him and God," they write.

Spectators are indifferent or "spiritually neutral," neither hostile nor skeptical. The Strobels write, "Because spectators don't recognize the relevance of God to their lives, it's helpful to get them thinking about matters of ultimate importance." Direct your conversations with a spectator to the meaning of life, destiny, purpose, and eternity.

Seekers are open, willing, and eager. God is active in opening the spiritual eyes and ears of a seeker. If your husband is showing signs of interest, encourage him without steamrolling him with your enthusiasm and excitement. Give him the necessary time and space to come to his own acceptance of faith.

No matter what degree of openness, no matter what "species" your husband may be, the best thing you, as his wife, can do is to keep your focus on Jesus and not on your husband's progress or lack of it—and pray, pray, pray.

Lord,
At one time I was a skeptic,
And you quelled my doubts, calmed my fears, answered
*   my questions.*
I was a spectator,
And you captured my attention;
You put eternity in my heart.
You set your affection on me;
You moved in my heart and caused me to seek you
When I wasn't even interested.
So I know, Lord, that you are more than able
To change my husband's heart and mind,
No matter what his degree of openness.
I don't have to worry because no "species" is too hard for you.
Give me discernment and wisdom
To aid my husband in his own faith journey,
And patience to deal with him along the way.
Amen.

ENVY ROTS THE BONES

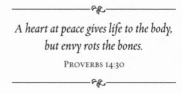

*A heart at peace gives life to the body,
but envy rots the bones.*

PROVERBS 14:30

E nvy is one of those troubling emotions that sneaks up from behind and clobbers you until you're blind. A friend told me recently about her struggle. She said, "My church is active and alive and growing by leaps and bounds. The gospel is sweeping through my community and gripping entire families. Yet I sit there by myself, week after week, watching the rows of pews fill with husbands and wives, in-laws and children, while the seat next to me stays empty.

"I don't go to church expecting to get clobbered, and most weeks I guard myself with things I know are true: God is sovereign; he knows and hears my prayers; he will meet all my needs. Most weeks I'm able to enter into worship and enjoy the people around me. But every once in awhile, my mind and my eye will wander to a family, and envy will blind me to everything else. *Look at them holding hands. It's not fair.*"

She said she starts dwelling on what others have and what she doesn't have until envy starts eating at her and "rotting her bones."

Envy, if left unchecked, leads to bitterness, "disorder and every evil practice" (James 3:16). At its core, envy doubts God's

159

goodness. It tells God, "All that you have graciously provided me is not enough."

God has been good to each one of us. He is the One whom the psalmist said does not withhold any good thing from those whose walk is blameless (Psalm 84:11). If we will remember that and recount all the ways he continues to show his goodness, envy changes to contentment, our sight is restored, and our rotting bones are healed.

Lord,
You know how I long for my whole family
To share a heritage of faith.
I want my family to fill an entire row at church!
"Me too, Lord!" my heart cries. "My turn!"
You also know
How prone my heart is to envy those around me.
It's not that I wish them evil,
I just want what they have.
I confess my envy as the sin that it is
And humbly ask that you fill my heart and my mind
With the knowledge of your goodness to me,
That I may be content,
That even my contentment may bring glory to your name.
Amen.

HE'S OF
ANOTHER FAITH

---

*I am the way and the truth and
the life. No one comes to the
Father except through me.*

JOHN 14:6

Margaret and her husband were pillars of their church in New England. She had thought she was a Christian until someone shared the gospel with her, and her eyes were opened. She saw that her religion and her church's beliefs were not biblical. Instead, they followed the teachings of a person and an incorrect interpretation of the Scriptures.

To Margaret, becoming a Christian meant a radical change in her beliefs. However, her husband thought their church was basically the same as biblical Christianity, and he wanted them to continue attending the church where they had made close friends. He wanted to maintain their status, but she wanted to go where she would be fed the truth.

What do you do when your husband is religious but not Christian?

In their book *Surviving a Spiritual Mismatch in Marriage,* Lee and Leslie Strobel advise wives to become educated about a husband's religious beliefs—where they are similar and where they differ from Christianity.

As they point out, "While there are irreconcilable differences between all other religions and Christianity—since Christianity is built around the uniqueness of Jesus as the Son of God and the 'Done' rather than the 'Do' plan of salvation—there may nevertheless be some similarities in certain basic values, such as honesty, integrity, concern for the poor, and so forth. Helping identify these commonalities can validate your faith in his eyes and possibly make him open to Christian training for your children, where such values can be inculcated."

While it's important to be tolerant of a husband's beliefs, the Strobels warn against compromising the truth. Not all religions lead to heaven, as some believe, only faith in Jesus alone. However, a husband's different religious beliefs can serve as a starting point toward his eventually finding the Way.

> Lord,
> Once I was blind, but now I see—
> And now I see clearly.
> How amazing is your grace toward me
> To open my own eyes to my spiritual blindness.
> I ask for that same grace for my husband.
> Open his eyes to the truth of your gospel and the error of
>   his beliefs.
> Help me to be tolerant but not compromising
> And as patient with him
> As you have been with me.
> Open his eyes, Lord,
> That he may see Jesus!
> Amen.

HOW LONG
UNTIL . . . ?

---

*But do not forget this one thing,
dear friends: With the Lord a day
is like a thousand years, and a
thousand years are like a day.*

2 PETER 3:8

When I first became a Christian, I sought out every woman at my church with a once-unbelieving-now-believing husband and implored, "How long did it take? How long did you pray?"

I'd listen to testimonies and try to calculate how long it might be until my own husband came to faith in Christ. I hated hearing people tell me things like, "My grandmother prayed for my grandfather for forty years before he became a Christian." To me, that wasn't encouraging at all. I wanted to hear the quickie salvation stories because that's what I wanted to happen at my house.

So I kept one eye on my husband and the other on the calendar, which meant I had no eyes on the Lord. As a result, I was anxious and impatient, driving myself and my husband crazy. He knew I was hoping he would accept Christ "soon," and he also knew he wasn't ready. I seemed to be the only one who didn't know that.

As time went on and I grew more anxious, a woman at my church told me, "You need to plan for the long haul. This could take a lifetime, and you need to be prepared. Besides, God has his own timetable, and you can't change it."

I was taken aback by her bluntness, but then I remembered it was her grandmother who had prayed for forty years.

Now, two decades later, I realize that was some of the best advice I ever received. By taking my eyes off the calendar and off my husband's "progress" and putting them on God (where they belong), I've been able to relax.

Long ago I decided that if it takes twenty, forty, or eighty years until my husband is ready to bend his knee, then I don't want to waste those years being anxious about something I have no control over anyway. Instead, I want to spend my years enjoying God and enjoying my husband, too. Meanwhile, I keep praying, and if my prayers are answered sooner than later, then that's icing on the cake.

Lord,
When I keep my eye on the calendar
Or put my hope and base my happiness on "signs" of
*   my husband's progress,*
Then I make his salvation my god.
But you alone are God,
And salvation comes from you,
Not from my persistent watching and anxious waiting.
Because you're not in any hurry,
Because you are Almighty God,
I can wait.
Hallelujah, I can rest.
Amen.

WITH EYES
WIDE OPEN

As far as the east is from the west,
so far has he removed our
transgressions from us.

PSALM 103:12

Carrie said she couldn't shake her guilt. "I've been a Christian for five years and married for two. What can I say? I married an unbeliever anyway," she said.

She said that most of the women she knows who are in spiritually unequal marriages came to faith in Christ after they were married and that the books and advice for these women didn't adequately address her situation.

Although I didn't know her well, I could see that the guilt of her sin in marrying a non-Christian with her eyes wide open tainted her ability to receive God's grace for her. It was as if she felt she somehow didn't deserve the same grace that God gives to those who didn't "marry in sin."

I posed these questions to her: "Is there a sin that's too great for God to forgive? If so, is it your sin that's too great?"

She shook her head and said, "No."

"So if your sin is forgivable and God has forgiven it, does he take back his forgiveness?"

Again she said, "No."

I told her, "Even if you did marry in sin, God wasn't surprised. Not only that, he is more than able to take even your sin and use it for his glory and to refine your character."

No matter what we've done, once we belong to God, he takes our sin and removes it "as far as the east is from the west." He chooses to remember it no more and refuses to hold it against us. And if he doesn't hold it against us, who are we to do so?

Once we are forgiven, we are free from the penalty of our guilt. God offers us his grace so we can walk in that freedom. All we have to do is receive it—with eyes wide open.

Father,
When I think of my sin,
My guilt cripples me.
Over and over I beg for your forgiveness,
And although you freely and lavishly extend it,
I too often choose to hobble along,
Guilty,
Rejecting the very forgiveness I've asked for.
How that must sadden you.
Though my sin may be great,
Your grace is far greater.
When I choose not to receive it,
I'm saying it's not enough.
Oh, Lord! I'm sorry.
You give grace, not because I deserve it,
But because I need it. I need it!
Oh, Lord! How I need it!
Amen.

"The Only Way Out Is Through"

—⁂—

*Each one should remain in
the situation which he was in
when God called him.*

1 CORINTHIANS 7:20

—⁂—

When my older daughter was first married, she went to join her Army husband in Missouri. While they waited for housing to open up, they stayed with another couple in a one bedroom apartment. They slept in the living room while the other couple and their baby and toddler slept in the bedroom; the only bathroom was also in the bedroom.

To make matters even more difficult, the Army base was in a desolate area, and they didn't have a car. My daughter felt trapped staying in that apartment day after day and called nearly every day, crying and begging to come back home so she could escape her difficult situation. Although it tore me up inside, I kept telling her no. "You need to be with your husband," I'd say. "You will get through this—I promise."

Maybe you've been toying with the idea of fleeing your marriage. You're tired of being "spiritually single." Maybe you can't see any signs of your husband showing even the faintest interest in your faith, let alone a faith of his own. To you, married life is a drudgery, an ordeal, and all you can think about is escaping.

But don't do it!

"If a woman has a husband who is not a believer and he is willing to live with her, she must not divorce him," instructs the apostle Paul (1 Corinthians 7:13).

For those going through tough times in marriage, author Bob Moeller in *For Better, for Worse, for Keeps* advocates holding fast to their wedding vows. "No problem can be solved by running from it . . . the only way out is through," he writes.

According to Moeller, the only way to fail in life or in marriage is to give up. But "if we keep getting up, coming back, and refusing to say 'die,' eventually we will prevail."

God never guarantees us a life without difficulties, only that we will be victorious if we hold fast to our faith, our hope, and our courage—and that we will make it through.

Lord,
I confess my thoughts of running out on my marriage
And giving up on my husband.
I confess that I want an easy way out.
But you've called me to persevere,
That it might build character,
And produce hope.
Hope!
That's what I need, Lord.
Hope to lift me out of my despair.
Hope to see the way through.
Hope to believe that you will use even this hard time for
*   my good—*
If I don't give up.
Help me, Lord, to not give up.
Amen.

WHAT'S RIGHT WITH
THIS PICTURE?

Whatever is true, whatever is noble,
whatever is right, whatever is pure,
whatever is lovely, whatever is
admirable — if anything is
excellent or praiseworthy —
think about such things.

PHILIPPIANS 4:8

If someone asked you to list everything you consider wrong about your marriage, how long would it take you to produce a ten-page document? How long would it take you to list just ten things you consider right about your marriage?

Most of us are much better at pointing out what's wrong with a situation that we find difficult than what's right with it. Living with an unsaved husband can be difficult at times, and for some it can be outright terrible, but it's a rare situation that's *all* bad.

The late Corrie ten Boom even found bits of joy in a Nazi concentration camp. In her book *The Hiding Place,* she writes about a "blessing" of fleas in the women's barracks. Corrie and her sister, Betsie, had been arrested, along with the rest of their family, for hiding Jews in their home in Holland. When the sisters arrived at Ravensbruck, they found nearly intolerable living conditions. Even so, these Christian sisters decided they would give God thanks—for being together, and for the fleas. Because the infestation was so bad, it kept the guards away, which allowed Corrie and Betsie the freedom to conduct nightly

169

worship services with the other women. In her world of darkness and grim misery, she knew full well what was wrong with her picture but chose to find something right.

Thinking about what's right about a situation doesn't mean discounting or denying what's wrong. It means keeping your eyes open to God's blessings and seeing his hand on your life—whatever is true, noble, right, pure, lovely, admirable, excellent, or praiseworthy—and thinking about such things.

Is your husband a good provider? Is he affectionate? Do you laugh together? Does he take care of your car for you?

By changing your focus from what's wrong with your situation to what's right, you'll be amazed at how much right you can find.

Lord,
Your grace reaches into the most difficult situations,
And it's your grace that opens my eyes to see
Right amid the wrong
And light in the darkness.
My husband may not share my faith,
But he's willing to share my life.
He provides for our needs and wants to spend time with me.
He respects my beliefs and encourages me to grow in my faith.
He loves me; he's proud of me.
I know, Lord, that there's more right with my picture than wrong,
But I didn't always think that way.
You opened my eyes; you lifted my head.
You haven't changed my situation, but you have changed my
*   heart.*
You have changed my attitude, changed my whole way of
*   thinking.*
You have changed my life!
Amen.

FROM VICTIM THINKING TO VICTOR LIVING

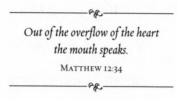

Out of the overflow of the heart the mouth speaks.

MATTHEW 12:34

"I'll never be able to do anything about my situation."

"My spouse is the problem."

"Nothing will ever change."

"Life's not fair."

Christian marriage and family counselor Dr. H. Norman Wright calls these "victim phrases." In *The Secrets of a Lasting Marriage* he says such phrases keep people prisoners in their own minds. By using them, we limit growth and change. They become self-fulfilling prophecies and lead to feelings of hopelessness, anger, resentment, bitterness, futility, and depression.

"What you *feel*, you will *say*—directly or indirectly—and your partner will probably respond in such a way as to confirm your worst thoughts about him or her," he writes. He adds that such thoughts create rather than solve problems. Negative thoughts become negative attitudes, which become negative actions, which kill a relationship. If you think your situation is hopeless, you'll stop trying, you'll stop giving. You'll quench the hope of the Spirit.

To combat "victim" phrases that creep into our thinking, Wright advises that we confront them by asking, "If I could change this negative thought into something positive, what would it be?"

Here are some examples:

"I'll never be able to do anything about my situation" can become "I can do all things through Christ. What can I do today?"

"My spouse is the problem" can become "How can I encourage him?"

"Nothing will ever change" can become "With God, nothing is impossible."

"Life's not fair" can become "What is God trying to teach me and how can I grow?"

What are some of the victim phrases in your vocabulary? By applying the uplifting promises in God's Word to your situation, how can you change your victim thinking into victor living?

Father,
What I think and what I speak
Is a reflection of what's in my heart.
When my heart is filled with victim phrases,
I think like a victim and act like a victim.
But in Christ, I am a victor, even in my marriage—
Especially in my marriage.
You "hold victory in store for the upright";
You are a "shield to those whose walk is blameless" (Proverbs 2:7).
You guard even me
And protect the way of those you have called to walk with you.
Forgive me for my victim thinking
And help me to live like the victor I am.
Amen.

MY ANXIOUS THOUGHTS, GOD'S FAITHFUL WORD

*... That through endurance and
the encouragement of the Scriptures
we might have hope.*

ROMANS 15:4

A few years ago a friend sent me an e-mail listing some of her anxious thoughts concerning her marriage to her unbelieving husband. She had been praying and waiting for nearly twenty-five years—more than half her life—and she was feeling discouraged as she started her list, but she was encouraged by the time she finished. She was encouraged as she found promises in the Bible that addressed each of her specific fears and anxieties. Here's what she sent me, plus I've added a few of my own:

It's impossible.

Nothing is impossible with God (Luke 1:37).

I can't do this anymore.

I can do everything through Christ (Philippians 4:13).

I'm tired.

God will give me rest (Matthew 11:28–30).

I feel unloved.

God has loved me with an everlasting love (Jeremiah 31:3).

I'm afraid.

God did not give me a spirit of fear but of power (2 Timothy 1:7).

I'm worried.

I can cast all my anxiety on God because he cares for me (1 Peter 5:7).

I'm lonely.

God says he will never leave me (Hebrews 13:5).

I'm impatient.

God isn't finished yet (Philippians 1:6) and isn't slow in keeping his promises (2 Peter 3:9).

I don't have enough faith.

To move mountains, all I need is faith the size of a mustard seed (Matthew 17:20).

I feel alone in my faith.

I belong to a family of believers (Ephesians 3:15).

I need hope.

The God of hope fills me with all joy and peace as I trust in him, so that I actually overflow with hope by the power of the Holy Spirit (Romans 15:13).

Father,
You are the God of comfort and encouragement,
The Lord of hope and peace.
When I am weak, you are my strength.
When I think I can't go on,
You tell me to keep going—
And then you pick me up and carry me.
You whisper to my heart, personally and intimately.
Because you are God
You know exactly what to say to meet my deepest needs.
Your Word lifts me; your holy Scriptures give me hope.
They are alive and give life to my anxious and weary soul.
How precious and faithful are your promises—and they're
    all for me!
Thank you, Lord, for your Word that revives me.
Amen.

Not Guilty

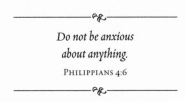

*Do not be anxious
about anything.*

Philippians 4:6

N ot one of us would come right out and say that we were
responsible for another person's salvation, but how many
of us secretly feel that way? It's subtle, but real. *If only I were a better Christian, he would see Christ in me and want to believe. If I
prayed more, if I was kinder, if I was more submissive, more loving. . . .*

We beat ourselves up, taking personal responsibility for a
husband's unbelief. To compound the guilt, often well-meaning
people at church say things like, "You just have to pray harder";
"Have more faith"; "Love him into the kingdom." Or they suggest that there must be some unconfessed sin in our lives. "Once
you get that under control, then God can work," they may insist.

But if salvation is a gift from God, if it's by grace that a person is saved "and this not from yourselves" (Ephesians 2:8), if no
one comes to Jesus without the Father drawing him (John 6:44),
then we're not responsible for a husband's—or anyone else's—
salvation. We can be influential, but ultimately it's between God
and an individual. When and if a husband comes to faith does
not depend on what we do or don't do, how hard or how long
we pray, how submissive we are or how well we love.

As a friend once (bluntly) put it after I had woefully con-
fessed the guilt I felt over my failure to influence my husband for

Christ, "You give yourself too much credit. Since when did you become God?"

The truth is, we are not responsible for another person's eternal destiny, and any guilt we feel is not from God. And if the guilt is not from him, then it's not real—and we are *not* guilty.

Case closed.

Father,
Sometimes I feel as if the destiny of the entire world,
Or at least the people in my world,
Rests on my shoulders, and I'm crushed by the weight.
When I don't see progress,
When my husband seems to go further away from Christ,
I can't help thinking that it's my fault.
But it's not my fault! That's a lie.
The truth is, you are God and I am not.
Salvation is yours to give, in your time, in your way.
You never intended for me to carry this burden;
You never said my husband's salvation is dependent on
      my performance.
Oh, may my heart believe that!
May this guilt I feel be lifted from me
So that I may walk in freedom,
For you have set me free.
Amen.

WOULD I LIKE TO
BE MARRIED TO ME?

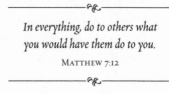

*In everything, do to others what
you would have them do to you.*

MATTHEW 7:12

Not many of us would welcome our lives being videotaped,
but it might be a good idea. I remember a TV news pro-
gram that filmed several couples in their homes for several days.
The couples had volunteered for the challenge because they
acknowledged that they had problems in their marriages and
thought the tapes might reveal some clues.

When the couples viewed the tapes of themselves, they were
speechless. Not one of them was prepared for the reality of their
nagging, their finger-pointing and blaming, their yelling and
belittling. More than one person exclaimed, "I know that's me,
but that's not me!"

But it was them, and they couldn't deny it.

If you were to watch a tape of your interaction with your
husband, what would it reveal? What would it be like to be married to you?

Are you a nag? *How many times do I have to ask you to take out
the trash? You said you would come to church with us this Sunday.
The front door knob is still loose—did you forget?*

Do you resort to blame? *If you would show more interest in the
kids, maybe they wouldn't whine so much. If you had a better job,*

177

maybe we could get out of this dump. If you'd get your life right with the Lord, we wouldn't have all these problems.

We are called to be kind and encouraging, to speak with grace and live humbly—not as doormats without opinions and input, but as respectful ministers of the gospel.

Do you want to be someone you would like to be married to? Then treat your husband as you want to be treated, which is no less than the Golden Rule. If you do, your life will shine brighter than gold.

Father,
I don't need a videotape of my life
To know I'm not the wife I should be—
My own conscience reminds me of that daily.
I hate the things that come out of my mouth!
I hate my attitude!
If I were my husband, I would hate being married to me.
All I can do, Lord,
Is to fall on my knees before you
And confess my desire to control my husband and our marriage,
To force things to be my way.
I know that when I do,
I'm not demonstrating the grace you've given me.
Help me to stop before I speak, to think before I act,
And to measure everything I do by your Golden Rule.
For your glory.
Amen.

PRAYING FOR
HIS REPENTANCE

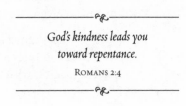

*God's kindness leads you
toward repentance.*

ROMANS 2:4

I n Western culture, men are taught to be self-sufficient, macho, tough, proud. "Big boys don't cry." Consequently, big boys also have trouble humbling themselves and admitting they're wrong, which is the first step to being reconciled to God.

In *The Power of a Praying Wife,* Stormie Omartian outlines three steps a person must take to change:

> Confession (admitting wrongdoing),
> Repentance (being sorry), and
> Forgiveness (being cleansed and released from guilt).

"The inability or resistance to do any of these three steps is rooted in pride," she writes. "Does your husband have trouble confessing his faults? Or is he the kind of person who can say 'I'm sorry' twenty times a day, yet the behavior he apologizes for never changes? In either case, he needs a repentant heart. . . . Only God can cause us to see our sin for what it is, and feel the same way he does."

When praying for your husband's repentance, in humility and deep concern ask God to:

- Open his eyes to his sin and take responsibility for it.
- Cause him to be sorry enough to want to change.
- Help him realize that he can't clean himself up.
- Remove his pride and give him a spirit of humility to ultimately receive Christ as his Savior.

The process of repentance is difficult, both for the one God is dealing with and the ones who stand by watching. It's not pleasant to be confronted with your own sin. But how glorious is the end result—clean hands, a clean heart, reconciliation with God, and life eternal.

Holy Father,
The things that make my husband successful in life—
His self-sufficiency and "I can do it" spirit—
Is also a big part of what keeps him
From humbling himself before you.
Lord, I confess that I'm sometimes afraid to pray for
     his repentance
Because I don't want him to suffer.
I don't want bad things to happen to him!
(I confess that I don't want the fallout—
When bad things happen to him, they happen to me, too.)
But you say that it's your kindness that leads to repentance.
In that case, I can be confident
That whatever it takes for my husband to repent
Will be from your kind hand.
Show him that humility is strength, not weakness,
And that repentance is not the end
But the beginning of life.
Amen.

GOD USES
UNBELIEVERS TOO

*I guide you in the way of wisdom
and lead you along straight paths.*

PROVERBS 4:11

A woman I know had been looking for a job and found herself with two offers and was unable to decide which one to accept. She said she had prayed about it but felt no clear direction from the Lord other than to ask her husband for his input.

However, she balked. "He's not a Christian," she told me.

As she and I prayed together, I asked God to speak to her husband and then have him tell my friend which job to take. Then I prayed that my friend would trust that her husband's answer was God's answer.

Although she was skeptical, she went home and asked her husband which job he thought she should take. He offered his opinion, and that was the job she accepted. Later she learned that the other company had decided to eliminate the job she had applied for.

As amazed as she was at God's using her husband to guide her, that was only part of the lesson the Lord had for my friend. She told me that her husband had said, "That's the first time you ever trusted me to give you advice. Just because I'm not a Christian doesn't mean I don't care about helping you. You finally gave me a chance."

To most men, when their wives ask for their advice, they interpret and receive it as respect and admiration. *She trusts me. I won't let her down.* Most men will rise to the occasion if they feel respected by their wives. Even most non-Christians want to do the right thing. It all boils down to trusting the Lord. That's what Queen Esther did when she approached the king with Haman's plot to kill her people. Because she trusted God as she presented her husband with the destiny of the Jews, an entire people was saved.

Lord,
I admit and confess that because he's not a Christian
I often discount my husband's advice.
But I'm wrong.
Unless what he tells me violates your Word,
It's your will for me
To submit to him,
To ask for his advice—and then to take it.
You who control the tides and direct the wind
Can certainly direct my husband's thoughts and counsel.
If I trust your bigness
And your loving care for me (and I do),
Then I can trust you to lead me in the way that you want me
*   to go,*
Even, and especially, through my husband.
Thank you for graciously setting him apart for your special
*   attention.*
Give him your wisdom, Lord, to lead me and our family.
I trust that you will.
Amen.

THE POWER
OF CHOICE

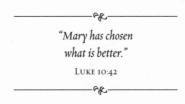

*"Mary has chosen
what is better."*

LUKE 10:42

I n *How to Act Right When Your Spouse Acts Wrong,* author and licensed clinical social worker Leslie Vernick poses a provocative way of looking at circumstances. She writes about a woman named Charlene who felt unhappy and bitter in her marriage. She felt victimized by her marital situation and by God.

"I'm a Christian. I *have* to stay," she said.

Vernick told her she didn't *have* to submit to her husband or stay in her marriage, and she didn't *have* to obey God or believe that his ways were good or right. Vernick also pointed out that she had the freedom to choose to not do the laundry or care for the kids. She could choose to quit her job and stay in bed all day. But because she didn't do any of that, she exercised her freedom of choice.

"By losing sight of her power to choose, Charlene robbed herself of the joy that comes from making good and right choices with a willing heart," Vernick writes.

Like Charlene, do you feel trapped? That's a common feeling for women in spiritually unequal marriages. They feel trapped by their circumstances, especially if they became Christians after they got married. *God, why didn't you save both of us at the same time? This constant tension isn't healthy for either of us—why don't you do something?*

God may not choose to "do something" right when we ask, but we can choose to do something about our attitudes. We can choose to feel trapped by circumstances, or we can choose to believe that we stay because it's the right thing to do and that God will meet our needs.

We are not powerless in our situation. The power is in the choice.

Lord,
My circumstances may be out of my control,
But I can control my attitude.
You tell me in your Word
That my attitude should be the same as Jesus had:
Humble.
Other-centered.
Servant-like.
I can choose to act like a martyr
And be ruled by self-pity,
Or I can choose a better way—
The right way.
I choose it, Lord!
I choose it with joy
Because it's what pleases you.
Amen.

Stopping
the Drip

ᴏᵊ

A nagging wife annoys like
constant dripping.

PROVERBS 19:13 (LIVING BIBLE)

ᴏᵊ

Last week my husband was out of town, and I was left alone in the house with only a leaky downstairs toilet for company. It kept making a dripping noise, and I wasn't about to call the plumber and pay seventy-five dollars just to have him jiggle a handle or tighten a bolt—something my husband would do for free when he got home in a day or two.

Meanwhile, the constant dripping was beyond annoying. Even with the TV or the radio on, the dripping was all I could hear! If my husband hadn't come home early, I was ready to pay 7,500 dollars to get that dripping to stop.

The writer of Proverbs likens a woman's nagging to a constant dripping: irritating, annoying, grating. Nagging is especially irritating to a man. I remember hearing a man on the radio say that when a woman says something more than once to her husband, he perceives it as nagging.

Drip, drip, drip.

At its root, nagging (or fretting) is born of fear and is an attempt to control, to make sure everything turns out "right." As Les Carter writes in *Distant Partner,* many women fall into this habit in a search for affirmation, consideration, or cooperation. For the woman who nags her unbelieving husband about matters of faith, she does so with a legitimate concern for his spiritual condition—but it's still nagging.

185

We nag because we want results. Unfortunately, nagging never achieves the results we want. Instead, it makes husbands clam up, blow up, or run away. It causes men to tune out and harden their hearts. Carter tells women to go ahead and make their needs and wishes known, but by "*telling*, not *insisting* or even *imploring*. No crabbing, no justifications, no nit-picking. Send the ball to his court. If he returns, you're ahead. If he lets it by, you are no further behind."

Say *once*, matter-of-factly:

- "Honey, my car's making a funny noise. Will you check it out?"
- "When is a good night for us to go over the bank statements?"
- "Hey, Joe. There's a new Christian coffee house in town. Would you like to come with me Friday night?"

Above all, before one word leaves your lips, pray.

Lord,
It's not my words that is the problem,
But my heart.
My heart frets and wants what it wants,
And it wants to control;
It wants results—now.
I nag because I don't trust that you can—
That you will—change things.
That you will do something.
That's the real cry of my heart:
"Lord, do something!"
Lord, do something—in me.
Change my fretful, nagging heart.
And stop the drip, drip, drip.
Amen.

FALLING OUT OF LOVE

*What God has joined together,
let man not separate.*

MATTHEW 19:6

W hat do you do when you feel as if you have fallen out of love with your husband?" That was one of the questions posed to marriage and family therapist Dr. Leslie Parrott during an online chat sponsored by *Today's Christian Woman*. She said she loved that question because it hits all of us who are married.

Quoting from a Yale University study, she said love has three ingredients: passion, intimacy, and commitment.

Passion is the biological side of love. It flows with adrenaline and gets love going, but isn't good at keeping it going. Passion ebbs and flows.

Intimacy is the emotional side of love, the connectedness. Intimacy also ebbs and flows in marriage. This is the area most vulnerable for women in spiritually unequal marriages. When faith divides a couple, it divides the emotional connection. We no longer share the same values and point of view. Our interests are different, sometimes polar opposite.

Commitment is the foundation of love. Parrott said, "We have so many couples that come to us for counseling saying, 'I've fallen out of love.' What they're really saying is, 'I've lost the passion' or 'I'm feeling disconnected right now, missing the intimacy.' The truth is that there *is* an ebb and flow to these things, and if you hold on to the commitment, you can cultivate both passion and intimacy."

It's good to remember that God doesn't love us because we're so sweet and lovable that he can't help himself. He loves us with a covenantal, committed love that transcends feelings. And it's his commitment of love for us that enables us to hold fast to our own marriage commitments, even when the feelings aren't there.

Loving Lord,
I'm grateful that your love for me
Isn't dependent on feelings,
But on commitment.
I'm also grateful
That you know how fleeting my own feelings are,
And that my love for others,
For my husband,
Is often shallow—
Sometimes even nonexistent.
In these times when I feel
As if I've fallen out of love with him,
May you love him through me.
Use me, Lord, as your willing vessel,
For your love compels me.
Amen.

WHATEVER
IT TAKES

&

*Sometimes it takes a
painful experience to make
us change our ways.*

PROVERBS 20:30 (TEV)

&

Cheryl's husband called her one night from the county jail. He had been out drinking, and on his way home from the bar he ran a stop sign and plowed into the back of another car. No one was injured, but Dan was arrested for driving under the influence. He called Cheryl to ask her to bail him out of jail.

Cheryl had been praying for her husband, that God would get his attention and show him his sin and his need for the Savior. Up until then, Dan had lived a "charmed" life—everything had always gone his way. Now he was faced with going to court, being fined, losing his driver's license, maybe losing his job.

Immediately, Cheryl switched into her usual rescuer role and tried to figure out how she would get the necessary money for Dan's bail and get him out in time for him to get a few hours of sleep so he wouldn't miss work the next day. She even considered calling his boss to say Dan was sick so that he could stay home and rest. However, when she got into her car to go get him, the engine wouldn't start.

"Let me deal with him," she sensed the Lord tell her. Cheryl said she felt a strange peacefulness as she went back into the house and went to bed.

The next day Dan was released. He remained angry at Cheryl for weeks for not bailing him out and making things easy for him. "I thought you were a Christian," he told her.

Although letting Dan fall and suffer the consequences was agony, as Cheryl described, she remained firm in her commitment to let God "deal" with him, and she loved him as best she could without rescuing him. He did end up losing his job, and the court and lawyer fees wiped them out financially. But fifteen years later, Dan, now a committed and sober Christian, says it was the best thing that ever happened to him.

God doesn't always use painful circumstances to get a husband's attention, but sometimes he does. Either way, he is still sovereign. He is still God.

Sovereign God,
Perhaps the most difficult prayer is asking, "Do whatever
   it takes."
Sometimes "whatever it takes" is painful
For my husband and for me.
My husband's consequences affect me, affect our family.
When he falls, I fall too.
So I try to keep him from falling,
Instead of trusting that you may have a greater plan
To reach down into his lowest point,
Because you know that's where he needs to be
Before he'll respond to you.
So do your work, "whatever it takes."
I trust you, Lord.
Help me to trust you more.
Amen.

LIKE A DIAMOND
IN THE SKY

❦

*You will be a crown of splendor in
the LORD's hand, a royal diadem
in the hand of your God.*

ISAIAH 62:3

❦

As I started writing the last chapter of my book *When He Doesn't Believe,* I wanted it to be a chapter of hope. I knew I wanted to write about how a diamond is formed—how God takes a particle of carbon, one of the most common elements in the universe, and with intense heat and extreme pressure deep in the mantle of the earth creates a diamond.

I thought the message would be, "God can take an ordinary, even crummy, marriage, and with the intense heat and extreme pressure that often comes with a spiritual mismatch, turn it into a diamond." However, just as I started to write that, my universe fell apart. My husband was going through a time of depression, and he told me he thought it would be best for us both if we divorced.

Besides the thought of losing my husband of twenty-six years, I was faced with finishing a book that offered hope to women feeling hopeless in their marriages to unbelieving husbands. I felt I had absolutely nothing to offer, and I crumpled at the feet of Jesus to help me survive.

I don't know how God does what he does, but he moved heaven and earth to encourage and comfort me—and to help me write about diamonds and hope. I had realized that there are no guarantees in life. Even if a woman does everything perfectly, there's no guarantee that her husband will stay with her. Her marriage might never become a diamond—but she will. Every child of God will emerge from the heat and pressure of life like a diamond: durable, precious, and strong.

Several months later, my husband's depression ended, and we are still together, healthier and stronger than ever before.

And I am still, and always will be, a diamond, a royal diadem in the hand of my God.

Lord,
It's the difficulties of life,
The heat and the pressure,
That refine my character and make me strong.
Like a diamond formed by your hand
I reflect your light.
Through me, your brilliance and glory shine.
Do what needs to be done
In my life and in my marriage,
That I might be strong and indestructible
And sparkle and shine for you.
It's said that a diamond is forever.
I am yours forever, Lord.
That is my hope.
May your name be praised forever.
Amen.